A MAP OF LIFE

FRANK SHEED

A MAP OF LIFE

A Simple Study of the Catholic Faith

IGNATIUS PRESS   SAN FRANCISCO

Originally published by Sheed & Ward, London
© 1933 F. J. Sheed
Published with ecclesiastical approval

Cover art:
The Calling of Saint Peter
Daniel of Uranc (15th cen.)
Matenadaran Library, Yerevan, Armenia
© Scala / Art Resource, New York

Cover design by Roxanne Mei Lum

Reprinted with permission of W. Sheed
1994 Ignatius Press, San Francisco
ISBN 978-0-89870-474-7
Printed in the United States of America ∞

CONTENTS

INTRODUCTION

THE TRAVELLER through a strange country usually gets vivid impressions of individual things, but only a confused impression of the country in its totality. He remembers this mountain and that stream and the other village, but how one is related to the other, and the general winding of roads that he has barely glimpsed, cannot in the nature of things stand clear in his mind; and a map of the whole country seen at the end of his travels may very well be full of surprises and is, in any case, a totally new view. In very much the same way, a traveller through life gets vivid —sometimes extremely vivid—impressions of things near at hand, confused impressions of things seen at a distance or only heard of, but of the whole plan of life, no idea at all. In his mind will be a jumble of facts, tossed about in any order—God, sin, church-going, disease, sacraments, suffering, the treason of friends, hostilities, death and the fear of death, money and the loss of it, God-made-man—and so on without end. But which of these things are big things and which of them are little, he will not know with certainty: the things that have come nearest to himself will seem big things; the remoter things will seem small.

And of the relations of these things one to another— how one thing agrees with, or conflicts with, another —of all this, merely by dint of living, he will have only the most confused and uncertain impression. In fact, it may easily happen that a man who merely lives, and neither reflects nor is taught, does not even suspect relationships but thinks of all things as accidents with no reason in themselves save that they happened, and no connection with each other save that one came earlier and one came later. Because of this confusion, I propose to try to make what may roughly be called a map of life—a scale map in which the principal "natural features" will be shown in their right proportions and the roads between them drawn in. This map will *not* be of my own drawing, fruit of my own experience of life. Nor will it be of any man's drawing. It will be a transcript of what God, the Author of life, has revealed as to the meaning of the whole and the relations of the parts.

Nor will it be a demonstration. Maps do not prove, but only state. There are only two reasons for trusting a map: one is the authority of the map-maker: the other is one's own experience, when one has travelled the road with its guidance. The second is normally of less practical value. We need to be assured of a map's trustworthiness at the beginning of a journey. A map, therefore, must be accepted or rejected according to the confidence the map-maker deserves. In this instance, fortunately the map-maker is God. In this effort to set out the plan of life, there will be no attempt anywhere to prove the truth of what is said, but only to state what, according to the Church he founded, God *has* said.

I

THE PROBLEM OF LIFE'S PURPOSE

T O THE DETACHED OBSERVER, man is something of a curiosity. He lives in two worlds at once, and this not as a being who belongs to one world and has simply got tangled up in another, but as a being who belongs essentially to both of them. God, who alone exists in his own right, who is all-knowing and all-powerful, who exists without the shadow of limitation, made all things. Considering the beings God has made, we find two broad categories, spirit and matter.

Spirit is being that has the power of knowing and willing. Matter is being that has not these powers. There is a more obvious but less important distinction between them: matter can be perceived by the senses, spirit cannot.

Of God's creatures, there are some that are pure spirits—angels—with no material part. There are some that are purely material—animals, plants, stones, and the rest—with no spiritual part. Between them is man. In him alone spirit and matter are united: by his soul, he is a spirit as the angels are; by his body, he is part of the material universe.

And, as has already been said, he belongs to both worlds by his essence. He is not simply a spirit who is for the moment tied down to, or tied up in, a body. It is of his very nature to be a union of matter and spirit.

The soul of man is not more essentially a partner in the human compound than his body; but it is the more important partner. For, in the first place, it is the principle of life in the body: it remains with the body so long as the body is capable of being animated by it; the body corrupts, whereas the soul continues in existence. And in the second place, it knows and wills: that is, it has the two faculties of intellect and will by which it can enter into conscious and deter-mined relationship with all that is.

Such a being, then, is man. It is life *as it concerns man* that is the business of this map.

We shall understand the map better if we grasp its uni-versal necessity. A man may very well say that whether there is or is not a divine revelation as to the mean-ing of human life, it is at any rate only of academic interest, desired by none save the dwindling number who like things cut and dried and take comfort in the voice of authority.

For a man who reasons thus we must show that an acceptance of the revelation of God as to the meaning of life has a bearing not only upon holy living, but even upon sane living; that only those who believe in such a revelation can shape their own lives correctly or help their fellow men. Those who do not accept the revelation, even if they have the best will in the world (which not all men have), can neither direct their own lives aright nor help other men—save accidentally and within a very narrow field. From such men the world has little to hope and an immense amount to fear. And into their hands the world is tending more and more to fall. In a word, the reason for their helplessness, both in relation to themselves and in relation to others, is that they do not know what a man *is*.

You do not truly know what anything is until you know what it is *for*. Knowing what a thing is made of, even knowing whom a thing is made by, these things are but scanty knowledge, impotent of themselves to lead to fruitful action. The complete knowledge demands a knowledge of purpose. A very crude instance may make this sufficiently obvious truth still more obvious. Imagine a man who has never shaved and suppose that he suddenly discovers a razor. He does not know what it is, but he discovers that it cuts. Whereupon he uses it for cutting wood. He does not cut a great deal of wood and he ruins the razor, leaving it fit only for the scrap-heap. The point is that he has used it without knowing its purpose; and save by accident such use must always be misuse. And in the face of the general proposition that nothing can be used aright until its purpose is known, the man who uses anything at all without such knowledge is acting blindly. He may mean well, but meaning well is not a substitute for knowledge of purpose.

Obviously, the perfect way to know the purpose of a thing is to find out from its maker: any other method leaves too many loopholes for error.

Apply this principle to man himself: we cannot use ourselves aright nor help any other man till we know what man is for. We can meddle with him, tinker with him, mean well to him, but, save in a limited way, we cannot help him.

Here we must make a short digression. There are only two ways in which anything can come to be. Either it is intentional or accidental: that is, either someone intended it or it merely chanced. The thing that is intentional has a purpose; accidents have no purpose. Humanity, like other things, must be either an accident and so purposeless, or else have been made with intent. Catholics know that man was made, and made by an intelligent being who knew the purpose of his own action. Further, God who made us and knew what he made us for has told us what he made us for. Accepting his Word, we know the purpose of our existence, and we can proceed to live intelligently according to it. Short of this knowledge, intelligent living is not possible for us.

For apart from God's own statement as to what he had in mind when he made us, we have no way of knowing. We cannot tell ourselves: the scientist can tell us what we are made *of*—or rather what our bodies are made of—but he cannot tell us what we are made *for*; and by comparison with this altogether vital matter, what he has to say, interesting as it is, is but trivial.

In other words, short of *God* telling us, we cannot be told; and short of being told, we cannot know. We can of course theorize—or in plain English, guess. There is one, and only one, colourable alternative to a revelation from God as a means of knowing the purpose of man's existence. We might simply take human nature as it is, study it, come to a full and accurate knowledge of it; we could then reason from man's nature as to the particular purpose for which a being of that nature must have been made; or, avoiding the idea of purpose altogether, we might reason as to the best use to which a being of those powers could be put.

This, I say, is a colourable alternative. Indeed, for one who is unaware of the revelation of God, it is the highest exercise of the intellect. With this method, had God not told us what was in his mind, we should have had to rest content.[1] Yet we may be glad that he did not so leave us, since it is liable to error in many ways, of which two are of capital importance:

1. There may be error in the reading of human nature. Most of men's efforts to read human nature, and frame a system of life in accord with it, err by an inability to seize the whole. One part of human nature is isolated, the rest ignored. Further, as between various uses to which powers might be put, there can be no

[1] See Chapter 12.

deciding which is higher and which is lower, save in the light of the purpose of the whole being: those uses that serve the purpose are good, those that hinder it are bad.

2. The second objection is far more important and is, indeed, fundamental to the understanding of the whole of what is to come. Even if human nature were fully understood with no shadow of error, the purpose of man's life could be deduced from it only if the purpose of man's life were contained in it—that is, if man's purpose simply meant the highest activity possible to his own nature. But supposing the purpose of human life is some activity or state *higher than* man's nature. Then we cannot find it simply by studying his nature. And God has in fact taught that he destines us not for something of which our nature is in itself capable (and which might, therefore, as I have said, be deduced from our nature) but for something to which he in his generosity chose to lift us; and this obviously cannot be deduced from any study of us: one may deduce the incidence of justice, but not of generosity.

Given, then, that apart from the revelation of God we cannot know with certainty what is the purpose of our existence as man, the only thing left for the one who does not believe in such a revelation is to choose an object of life: to decide for himself what he will use his life for. But given the myriad possibilities before every man, the chances are that he will choose the wrong one and so spoil his life; and if he is in a position to control the destinies of others, whether as a king or a dictator or simply as the father of a family, the disaster will be very great—and the more zealous and energetic he is, the greater will the disaster be. In no case is intelligent living—that is, living consciously for the true purpose of our being—possible to us unless we are told by God what the purpose is.

It is, therefore, the very highest act of our intellect thus to grasp the revelation of God, since this is knowledge that we must have, and knowledge that we must either be told or do without. It is foolish to stigmatize this acceptance as a denial of freedom or a form of intellectual suicide. The object of thought is truth: if a particular piece of truth is necessary, can be known with certainty by the teaching of another, and cannot be known otherwise, then a man is really acting suicidally in rejecting the truth merely because he did not find it for himself. He is preferring the exercise of the means to the attainment of the end. If a man knows what knowing means, he cannot even think he knows man's true purpose save through the revelation of God. And so he cannot direct his own life rightly. Nor can he help others.

Here the philanthropist might say: "I am a practical man doing the immediate job. Whether there is a God or not, here is a man suffering, here is a wrong to be righted"; but this is not practical, this dashing at the job without the necessary preliminary theorizing. For if you do not know what men *are*—that is, are *for*—how do you know what is good for them? That thing is good for any being that helps it to achieve the true purpose of its nature. How can you help men to that if you do not know what their true purpose is?

Nor should we be misled by the fact that there are certain obvious things that such a man can do. Principally, he can relieve bodily suffering. But all his aid is "first aid"; of profound, permanent, certain help to man he can do nothing. In fact, the general effort of those who thus would help their fellow men with no thought of God is almost exclusively confined to bodily well-being or the relief of bodily suffering.

And when they approach such questions as birth control, divorce, the killing of the incurable, and a dozen others, it is beyond their power really to answer the question raised. For these things are right or wrong depending on whether they help or hinder a man in the achievement of the purpose of his being; and it is not so much as possible to express an intelligent opinion on them save in the light of a sure knowledge of what the purpose of life is. When the philanthropist is not merely unaware of God's revelation but definitely convinced that man is only the matter of his body, his position is easier. If he has to decide upon the question of divorce, for instance, then for him the only problem is whether an accidental collection of electrons and protons—called for convenience a man —will function more harmoniously with that second collection of electrons and protons it is at present living with or with some third collection of electrons and protons. Such a question is simple enough. Simple because it really does not matter. But if man is more than that—is a being with a true purpose in life —then all that is said in ignorance of his purpose is quite irrelevant.

On all the moral teaching of those who have not the Catholic revelation, there lies this mark of superficiality: the only rule that appears to be of universal application is that suffering must always be relieved. But even this, one dare not call a principle, since it is not related to any true view of life. By good fortune, it is a rule that often works to the advantage of the sufferer; and in the one who exercises it, it bears witness to a true virtue: indeed, the relief of suffering is one of the highest rules of the Christian life. But, apart from a right view of the purpose of human life, it is a blind rule, and there is no virtue in blindness. Carried too far, as our age is tending more and more to carry it, the rule can work immeasurable evil. For there are things that are worse than suffering.

Two questions, then, are to be asked of any religious or social teacher who offers some system of life for the acceptance of men: The first is: What, according to you, is the purpose of man's life? The second is: How do you know? When he answers the second, be very insistent. Unless he says "God has revealed it", then he is wasting time. If he says God has revealed it, then he must be prepared to show that God has done so. To both questions, the Catholic Church has an answer. In this book, I am concerned only with the first and with certain things that flow from it. Life, and all the things of life, have a meaning in relation to man, in themselves, in relation to one another. What the meaning is, God has told us: we need to know it; there is no other way of knowing. This book is simply an attempt to transcribe what God has said.

2

THE PROBLEM OF LIFE'S LAWS

THE ARGUMENT of the first chapter went to show that the very minimum required for intelligent living—namely, the knowledge of the purpose of our life—is dependent upon a revelation from God, that without such a revelation we cannot know our purpose and so cannot have any means of testing the value or the significance of anything that we do. As I have said, this is a minimum, and reflection on experience is sufficient to show that something more is needed from God than a bare revelation of what he made us for.

Very early in life, man becomes aware that he is living in a world of laws: the series of happenings that lead him to the conclusion are nearly all unpleasant; but whether he ever formulates the idea or crystallizes it in a word or whether he remains merely the practical man—in the usual sense of the unreflective man— he acquires the certainty that there is a whole series of conditions and results in the world that may fairly well be counted upon. This certainty becomes part of the very texture of his mind. Thus he discovers that fire burns, that hunger weakens, that rain wets, that bodies fall toward the earth and not toward the sky, and so with a myriad other things. If he reflects at all upon these laws, he realizes that they are not of his choosing—in fact that, in many cases, they are the reverse of what he would have chosen—but that their power is in no way affected by his disapproval. There is no way in which he can get free of them. He can act as though they did not exist, in which case they damage or even destroy him. If he is a sane man, he may dislike them but he accepts them and does his best to live in accordance with them. In any case, there is no such thing as freedom *from* them, but only freedom *within* them. And freedom within them can be attained only by one who knows them. This knowing them is always a matter of discovery and not invention; in other words, one finds out what they are, one cannot in any way make them to be.

All this is obvious enough as applied to the body. Men, however, do not always make the application of precisely the same truths to the soul; yet the parallel is exact. As there are laws that govern the body, so there are laws—in particular the moral law—that govern the soul. The moral law is no more made by man, or dependent on the approval of man, or in any way escapable by man than the material law. Man can *ignore* the moral law as he can ignore the material law, but the result in both cases is his own diminution or destruction. There is no freedom from the moral law;

but as with the material law, there is freedom within it, the only freedom possible to man. And a condition of this freedom is the same as in the other case—namely, knowledge of what the law is.

In the light of all this, it is possible to judge the extent of folly of those who talk of emancipation from the moral law, or from any particular article of the moral law; and because this talk has folly at its root, it runs to folly in every leaf and flower. To take only one instance: one hears the phrase that the modern man is no longer to be bound by the two-thousand-year-old law of marriage. It is as though one were to say that it was beneath the dignity of modern man to be bound by the even older law of gravity. For the question is not whether the law is old, but whether it is a law. A man might very well say that he would not be bound by the law of gravity, yet he would be well advised to keep his affirmation within the sphere of words. Let him push it to act, and he will no longer be a modern man but a corpse, part of that history that, in his newness, he so heartily despises.

Another category of this folly is the not uncommon assumption that this or that human *authority* may abrogate the law, even if the individual would be a little reckless in declaring it not binding upon himself. But the state—to take the most obvious example of all —cannot in any way affect the moral law.[1] The state declares that a man may—in certain circumstances—

---

[1] Nor can the Church. See page 103.

leave his wife and marry another. But this is adultery. To assume that therefore adultery is no longer harmful to the soul is unduly optimistic. State action can no more make adultery harmless to the soul than it can make prussic acid harmless to the body. Men have come into a collision with the law of God: the law of God does not suffer from the collision.

The conclusion, then, is that we are living in a world of law—material law and spiritual law—and that successful living involves obedience to this law, which, in its turn, supposes a knowledge of it. If it is asked how we are to know what the law is, experience suggests an answer. Since men were men, they have had their own bodies and the world of matter under their eyes, and they have been at work discovering what the laws are that govern matter. Yet on this most obvious ground, men are constantly changing their views, learning laws that till yesterday were not so much as suspected, discarding what all men before them had held to be laws, certain and irrevocable. So that it is clear enough that, left to themselves, men will make no more than a tolerably successful job of this discovering of the laws of matter. Much more, then, it is evident that left to themselves, men will fail to discover, with any fixity or certainty, the laws that govern the soul—since the soul is so much less obvious to man, so very much more inaccessible in its essential being. And failure in this sphere is far more serious than in the other. For disaster to the body is the lesser evil and is only an anticipation of the disaster that awaits all bodies inevitably.

But disaster to the soul—because it is the nobler part of man, because disaster is not its inevitable destiny, because it is not only the nobler part but the decisive part—is a thing not to be faced. And, in fact, given that no one but the law-maker can know with certainty the text of the laws he has made, there is immense food for thought in this: that God, the Author alike of the laws that govern matter and the laws that govern spirit, has left man very largely to discover—with an endless accompaniment of disaster—the laws that govern matter, as though the discovery of these were a trivial thing, not vital; but has revealed to man the laws that govern spirit because they are essential laws, whose breach is fraught with eternal catastrophe.

Thus, not only that man may know the *purpose* of his life, but also that he may know the *nature* of the life through which he must strive to his goal, a teaching from God is something vitally necessary. It does not follow that even with this knowledge a man will always act rightly. The *will* of man is capable of choosing a course of action contrary to what he knows to be right. And even if the will is right, the *intellect* may err in applying its knowledge of purpose and law to a particular set of circumstances. Where the law of God applies explicitly, there is no problem. But in a situation to which the law has not been applied by God in express terms and it is a question of men applying a principle, then they may easily go astray, misled by custom or environment or inclination. Thus, for example, a Catholic might, with excellent intentions, support a bad social or economic or judicial system. But for all that, he possesses the true principles, and with these, there is always the possibility of rectification. Without them there is none. So that right living —though not guaranteed by—is yet totally dependent upon knowledge of purpose and law—and therefore upon God.

It may be well at this point, to say one thing further about freedom and about the dependence of man upon God. Freedom is usually defined as the power to do what one likes. Accepting the definition, one sees instantly that the power to do what one likes may be the goal, but doing what one likes is not necessarily the road to the goal. In the bodily order, eating what one likes, for instance, may very well be the very solidest hindrance to doing what one likes and a certain prelude to suffering what one very much dislikes. It is only by doing as one ought that one attains a condition in which one has true physical freedom, the uttermost freedom possible to the body. And the same truth applies exactly to the soul. Freedom, then, is not to be attained by doing what we like unless by chance we like what we ought, which brings us back to the true purpose of our being and the laws by which our being may progress toward it. Apart from that is only loss.

It is true that this argues a very extreme degree of dependence upon God, a dependence to which not all men resign themselves easily. Yet no view of life

will work—because no view of life is intelligent—
that does not accept both the fact of our dependence
upon God and the rightfulness of it—that God has no
duty whatever to us, and we have no rights whatever
against God. If a carpenter makes a chair, the carpenter owes nothing to the chair. The chair has no rights
against him, and he may do as he pleases—sit upon it
or set a match to it. But God made us and he made us
more fully, so to speak, than any carpenter ever makes
a chair. For the carpenter, at any rate, does not make
the wood, and there is always the possibility that his
rights over the chair may, to some extent, be limited
by an unpaid bill for the wood. But God made us,
using no material at all. Therefore, we have no more
rights against him than the chair has against the carpenter. Occasionally, it seems to us that the fact that
we have intelligence and free will does, in some way,
make a difference, giving us some claim that the chair
has not. But God gave us these gifts too; they are as
much his creatures as we, and, therefore, they give us
no claim against him. God could not contract a duty
toward us by giving us more. But though God has
no duties toward us, yet he has a duty toward himself,
the duty of acting intelligently. Intelligent action means
action with a purpose, and God who gave us intelligence and gave us free will thereby put himself under
obligation, so to speak, to treat us in accordance with
that which he had given us. Our dependence, therefore, upon God, though total, absolute, and without
any shadow of exception, is not the dependence of

machines upon a mad mechanic or of slaves upon a mad king. It is the dependence of free men upon an all-wise and all-loving Creator, who knows their being more intimately than they know it themselves—who knows wherein the fulfillment of their being lies, and whose will it is that the fulfillment should actually be achieved. As we shall see, his will for them is even more than that—a fulfillment immeasurably beyond anything that the mere powers of their being would lead men to dare to hope—or even to conceive.

3

HEAVEN

I N THIS THIRD CHAPTER, we come at last to the map itself, or rather to a first general outline of it. We must begin at the end. For this map is the map of a road, and it is only in the light of its end that any road makes sense. If you ask why it turns this way or that, the answer will always lie in a consideration of the place it is going to: till you know that you cannot even know that it is a road, but only that it looks like one; still less can you know whether it is a good road or a bad road. Therefore, if this map is to be drawn rightly, we must begin at the end.

What is the right end of the life of man? In other words, what should the road of life lead to? Faced with this primary question, men have tried various ways of arriving at the answer. The atheist makes an effort to place the end of the road at death: the road of every man's life runs inevitably to earth in a newly opened grave. But atheists, at any time in the world's history, are exceptional, almost freakish. And for the generality of men, the question of what is the end of life is simply the question of what comes after death. In this at any rate, the generality of men are right. But after this initial correctness there is every variety of error. Some men have decided to work out for themselves what they think lies on the other side of the door of death, with the ill-success that must always attend any effort to arrive theoretically at a true idea of an unvisited country. Some have decided that whatever lies on the other side of the door, there is no need to worry about it, but merely to await death and hope for the best with a fair certainty that things will turn out well enough. A small number—even smaller than the number of atheists perhaps—have, in all ages, tried to find out by consulting the souls of the dead, which, logically, is at any rate a far better method than merely theorizing about the life after death. For all that, the method is fraught with endless danger of deception, and for all the thousands of years of its history, the results are so meagre that spiritualism can hardly be conceived as anything more worthy than a kind of peeping through the keyhole.

The Catholic has always realized that as to what comes after death, the only way of finding out is to be told by someone who has personal knowledge of the other world. No other way could possibly be right. So far the spiritualist has hold of a truth. But of all the beings who may have such personal knowledge, one has it supremely—God. And God, the Author of this life and the next, has told us of the future that he has prepared for us. The road of life runs through this life to heaven. Heaven, then, is the end of the road, and we can only understand the road if we have some knowledge of heaven, the place to which it leads and for which it was made.

At this stage, no more will be said of heaven than is necessary for the mapping of the road. A slightly fuller treatment of heaven, in its own right and not simply as something that makes this life on earth comprehensible, must be reserved for the final chapter.

Outside the Catholic Church, the idea of heaven has suffered because the only section of Protestants who talk very much about it—Protestants of the Nonconformist type—having no theology on the subject, have been forced more and more to use the imagery of Scripture. For centuries, they have talked, preached, and sung of heaven as a place of harps, hymns, crowns of gold, streets of jasper. These, of course, are symbols intended to convey a vivid impression of endless happiness. In themselves, they give no notion of the life of heaven any more than pictures of men with wings give a notion of the being of angels. As symbols, they are made only as ornaments to a great body of teaching in which the life of heaven is expressed in its true relation to the nature of God and the nature of man. Lacking this true teaching—owing to its suspicion of "theology"—Protestantism has for centuries had no food for its mind save the symbols; and symbols, while an admirable stimulus to the imagination, are not food for the intellect. The result is that for the average man, heaven, thought of in terms of endless hymn-singing, is not attractive.

For the moment, then, we must neglect the symbols altogether. Heaven consists in the knowledge of God and in the love of God, flowing from and proportioned to that knowledge. As such, it means perfect happiness. If we consider what brings happiness to man in this life, we shall find certain very clear principles: happiness is always in the soul; it may be caused by some condition of the body, but the body as such is neither happy nor unhappy. It is the soul that knows of the good or ill condition of the body and rejoices in the good or suffers in the ill. In that happiness of the soul that comes from some condition of the body, the condition always is that the bodily organs are functioning properly. Let them cease to do so, and the state of the soul that we call "unhappiness" is nearly certain to result in some measure; not quite certain, be it noted: the soul can triumph even over the body's agony. This fact, that the soul is the seat of happiness, is further shown when we consider a situation in which the body is functioning properly, but the soul itself is perturbed. In such a situation, the state of the soul is decisive: the man is unhappy. A very simple instance is where the man has all, not only that he needs, but even that he wants to drink and eat and wear and entertain himself with. The death of a friend is instantly sufficient to plunge him into the deepest unhappiness. That being so, it is necessary to consider in what lies the happiness that comes from the soul itself.

Like that which comes from the body, it always results from a proper functioning of a faculty. The intellect knows truth and is happy in the knowledge: the
will loves goodness and is happy in the love. The soul
of man sees and rejoices in beauty: beauty of sound,
beauty of colour, beauty of form—above all, beauty
of spirit. In heaven, all this is carried to its very highest point. The intellect, whose property it is to possess the knowledge of truth, now knows God himself,
who is supreme Truth. The will, whose property it is
to love goodness, is now in immediate contact with
God himself, who is supreme Goodness. The whole
soul is therefore functioning at its very highest, and
happiness is the inevitable result.

Our imagination may find in this statement—that
the happiness of heaven consists in the direct knowledge and direct love of God—a doctrine that it feels
to be deeply unsatisfying. To the ordinary man, such
a description of heaven seems far too spiritual, too remote from the kind of happiness that springs to his
mind the moment he starts to think of happiness at
all. It is, therefore, well to analyse just one stage further what happiness involves. In looking at a sunset
or in listening to a piece of music, the soul of man
may be lifted, if only for the moment, to an absolute
ecstasy of happiness. Yet no man can go on endlessly
looking at the same sunset, and an endless repetition
of the same piece of music might very easily lead to
madness. Both these effects, the original joy and the
too rapid fatigue, come from the same source. The

beauty that man enjoys in the sunset and the music, is a beauty that God himself has created, and it is to this that the soul of man responds. But, because God has created it, it is only a shadow or a reflection of that beauty that, immeasurably, is in God himself, or more truly is God himself. Man, therefore, who has rejoiced in the beauty that God has placed in the sunset, will rejoice immeasurably more in God himself, the Author and Source of all beauty. And whereas he grew weary of the sunset—which was not the beauty of God himself, but only a created reflection of it—of the infinite beauty of God himself he will never grow weary.

The Supernatural Life

This, then, is some idea of the end of the road; what bearing has it on the road? To many, the connection is obscured by a truth that is only one truth, and not the most important. Heaven is thought of as the reward of a good life. As such, it has only a kind of accidental connection with this life. It is better to think of heaven, not only as a reward, but also as the *result* of a good life. A simple comparison may make clear the distinction. If a student passes an examination, he may be rewarded in one of two ways: he may either get a mere prize—a tennis racquet say, or a volume of Browning—or he may be admitted to a further course of study that his success in the examination has proved him to be fitted for. The tennis racquet has no real re-

lation to the examination he has passed, but the further course of study has; it is a true result of it. To an
immense number of people, heaven is rather like the
tennis racquet, and, as such, is not really understood
at all. But think of it as the further course, resulting
from a life well lived, and instantly the connection is
seen. This life is not only a test that a man must pass
in order to obtain the reward of heaven, it is also a
preparation a man must successfully undergo in order
to live the life of heaven.

From this, it follows that whatever is necessary to
enable a man to live the life of heaven must, in some
way or other, be acquired by man in this life: otherwise this life would not be a preparation for heaven.
And this consideration brings us to the most important
point in the whole of Catholic teaching, the doctrine
to which all others whatsoever are related, an understanding of which is necessary if Catholicism is to be
understood at all. We may approach it in this way. If
we were offered a journey to another planet, we should
be wise to refuse, because the breathing apparatus we
have by nature was made for the atmosphere of this
world. In our atmosphere it works; in a totally different atmosphere it would not work, and we should die
of suffocation. This illustration points the way to the
truth, namely, that the equipment that is adequate to
life in one world may not be at all adequate to life in
another. And God has told us that our human nature,
while adequate to the ordinary life of this world, is not
adequate to the life of the world to come. If we were

to enter heaven with only the powers of our human
nature, we should no more be able to live there than,
in the illustration I have given, we should be able to
live on another planet with no powers beyond those
of our nature.

And just as we should need some extra powers of
breathing not contained in our nature, to live on another planet, so we need extra powers in our soul,
not contained in our nature, in order that we may live
the life of heaven. These powers not ours by nature,
which are necessary in order that we may live a life
totally above our nature, are what is called in Catholic
teaching, the Supernatural Life.[1]

All that has just been said of man applies equally to
those purely spiritual beings, the angels. Heaven consists in such a relationship with God that no created
nature, by its own powers, could be adequate to it.
Just as men must receive powers above their nature
if they are to live the life of heaven, so must angels.
Angels had their testing. Those who remained in the
love of God were granted the powers and admitted to
heaven. Those who rejected God were fixed in eternal
separation from him.

But as we have already seen that our life upon earth
is to be a preparation for the life of heaven, and that

[1] Not, be it noted the *spiritual* life, though in Scripture this term
is often used for the Supernatural Life. It seems better here to keep
the terms distinct. Man's soul is by nature spiritual. The Supernatural
Life is something that elevates spirit.

heaven is to be the logical conclusion of this life, and that, therefore, whatever is necessary to the life of heaven must be acquired by us here—because of all these things it follows that in this life we must obtain from God the Supernatural Life.

Our life will be a success if, at the moment of death, we have in our soul the life above our nature, the Supernatural Life. It will be a failure if, at death, we have not the Supernatural Life. For if we have it, then we have in our soul the powers that would enable us to live the life of heaven; if we have it not, we lack these powers and therefore will be totally unable to live the life of heaven. The road of our life, then, will lead us to heaven only if on it we have acquired the Supernatural Life, and at the end of it, have retained the Supernatural Life.

This, then, is the first general outline of our map. There is a road leading man to that ineffable intimacy with God that we call heaven. The condition of walking the road aright is the Supernatural Life. It will be seen how every single thing that happens to man has its bearing on this Supernatural Life and is a good thing or a bad thing depending on whether it helps it or hinders it. Every single doctrine of the Catholic Church is bound up with this, and every single practice of the Catholic Church is concerned with this and with nothing else, and apart from this, has no meaning.

4

THE CREATION AND FALL

WE HAVE NOW SEEN the right road in its simplest elements. Our entry into life is at one end; heaven is at the other; death lies between. To understand the map, we need a knowledge of the purpose of life and a knowledge of the laws to be obeyed; to put our understanding to fruitful use—that is, to attain the end for which we are made, we need the Supernatural Life.

These three things would be necessary, given a supernatural destiny, in any condition of the human race. And all of them must come as a free gift of God or not at all. For us, then, the question simply is: How does God give these gifts—the Life and the twofold Truth —to man here and now? The answer to this question is the actual road of today—life as it must actually be lived by ourselves. But we cannot understand the strange, winding, arduous, almost incomprehensible road of today unless we realize that it is not the first road God laid down for us, that in the beginning there was a simpler, less puzzling road, and that by sin man dynamited it; or from another point of view, man so damaged himself by sin that he could no longer walk it. A study of the first road and its ruin will make the road of today considerably more comprehensible.

From the first man, Adam, we all are sprung; in him, the whole human race was incorporated, since there is no one of us that does not come from him; he was the whole human race when God made him. He gave him, along with many other gifts, the three things necessary. He gave him the twofold Truth— the knowledge, that is, of the purpose of the human race and of the laws by which it must be governed if it is to avoid disaster. He gave him the Supernatural Life. Adam, then, had the natural life that made him man—the union of spiritual soul and material body that constituted his nature as man, without which he would not have been man; and this natural life he had in a state of perfection, all his powers and faculties rightly ordered, body subordinate to soul, soul ruled by reason. He also had the Supernatural Life—the life above nature—that whereby he would be able to live the life of heaven hereafter, whereby even in this life his whole soul was "supernaturalized", capable of a re- lationship with God altogether higher and holier than anything that could take its rise in man's merely natu- ral endowments. The highest and holiest point of this relationship and the very condition of the Supernatural Life was for Adam, as it is for all men, the union of the soul to God by love. And while he had the Supernat- ural Life, God also exempted his nature from the law of death—from the separation of soul and body that is the natural termination of man's life on this earth.

Now Adam is not to be thought of simply as an individual: he *was* the human race. God, then—in the very beginning, and, so to speak, as a matter of course —had conferred upon the human race the three gifts necessary. For Adam, the simplest elements of the road of human life were two, not three—his entry into life was at one end and heaven was at the other: death did not lie in between. That, simply and directly, was God's scheme: man had knowledge of the end of his existence, knowledge of the laws by which he might attain the end, the Supernatural Life that put the end within his power. And man wrecked the scheme. Adam sinned, rebelled against God, and thereby lost the Supernatural Life; for this life cannot exist where the love of God is not, and love of God cannot exist where there is rebellion against him.

Scripture represents the sinful action as the eating of the fruit of the forbidden tree. There is some mystery here. But two things about it we know. The first is that it was a sin of disobedience to God. The second is that the devil played a part in it. It has already been said that among the creatures of God were certain purely spiritual beings, the angels; and that these angels had the same purpose as man—to attain to heaven—and like man they had a period of testing. Some succeeded and are now in heaven. Some failed in the test, chose their own will rather than God's, and so lost heaven eternally. In the affairs of the human race, angels good and bad are mysteriously concerned. The good angels exercise a certain guardianship over men; the fallen angels—devils—are concerned in leading men into sin and so causing them to fail to reach heaven. The devil, then, tempted man to commit his first sin.

It is important to understand Adam's new condition. He had lost the Supernatural Life; he retained the natural life or the union of body and soul; the soul retained the natural powers of intellect and will. Supernaturally, he was dead, for the loss of life is death; naturally, he still lived. But even his nature did not emerge from the disaster unimpaired: it lost the privilege of exemption from death; henceforth, man must pass through the gateway of death to reach his eternal destiny. More serious still was that man's nature lost its *direction*. Adam had sinned because he had chosen his own will instead of God's—he had swung his nature out of its true Godward direction and had introduced war into the very inmost part of his nature, into the union of body and spirit—body warring against spirit, spirit torn by war in its own powers.

Thus then stood Adam, the *individual* man—the Supernatural Life lost, the natural life impaired because given a wrong direction; but still knowing the purpose of his being and the laws set by God for the governance of his life. But Adam was also, by God's dispensation, the *representative* man, and the effect of this original catastrophe upon the whole human race is measureless. As a mere physical consequence, the nature he had to hand on to his descendants was an impaired nature, strongly attracted to sin. Worse than that, the right relationship between God and the human race was broken, and heaven was closed to men.

In him, the race lost the Supernatural Life: so that men thereafter (with one glorious exception)[1] entered this world with the natural life of soul and body (so much was necessary that they should be of the human race), but without the Supernatural Life, which but for Adam's fall they would have had. This is what we call original sin, which is thus to be thought of not as a wrong done by us personally, not as corruption of the soul in its essence, but as the absence of that Life that makes us sons of God and will hereafter open heaven to us.

Thus then through the spoiling of God's plan, one of the three elementary things was lost—and lost instantly.

The other two were not lost so quickly. Adam we may assume, passed on his knowledge of God's purpose and God's laws to his children and they to their children. But as the slow centuries passed and men became further removed in time and space from the first revelation, that happened to it which must always happen to a tradition of men unguarded by God: error crept into it, passion distorted it violently, and self-interest less violently, but no less certainly; mere

[1] The exception was Mary, the Mother of Christ. From the first moment of her existence in her mother's womb, her soul possessed the Supernatural Life. This is called technically her Immaculate Conception.

forgetfulness was deadlier than all. The nature of man still bore witness to God's purpose and God's law—but a witness that grew ever fainter; the fragments remained of the first revelation—but ever more broken and shapeless; the little company of the Chosen People clung to certain fundamental truths—the oneness of God, for instance, and the certainty of a Saviour to come—but only under pressure of endless reminders from God and with heaven knows how much weariness and backsliding. And there came a time when the whole of the threefold gift almost seemed to have perished from the earth. The Life man had lost in one great catastrophe; the Truth man had frittered away. Men were born into the world without the Supernatural Life: with a nature hopelessly at war within itself. They could still, from the universe about them, reason to the existence of God. But even in this their reasoning was accompanied by a horde of errors, and they could have no certain knowledge of God's purpose or God's law. Chaos was upon them: their foot was upon a road whose end they did not know—a road that could only be travelled with aids that they did not possess and could not for themselves obtain.

And, be it repeated, heaven was closed to man. This is something different from having lost the Supernatural Life. For an individual might, by God's grace, regain the Supernatural Life; and yet because he was a member of a fallen *race*, he could not enter heaven. Man is not simply an individual, he is a member of a community. And while the only great human community in existence was Fallen Humanity—to which as a race heaven was closed—the individual, however holy, was debarred from heaven. Not till the right relation between God and the human race was reestablished (as God had promised Adam it would one day be) could the individual member of the race enter heaven. There was no question of course of a holy man being *eternally* debarred from heaven. But till heaven was reopened he must be in a place of waiting.[2]

At last God did for man what man could not do for himself: he made the threefold restoration and so built a new road for the human race; but consider what man had by his own act become, and it will be small wonder if the new road lacks some of the simplicity of the old. The first road had been planned for man as he came, all perfect from the hand of God; the second had to be planned for man as he was, with the wounds and stains that were upon him after countless ages of bearing the assaults of the world, the temptations of the devil, the warfare within himself. For the first road God had made man; for the building of the second road God *became* man.

[2] This place is referred to in various terms. Our Lord spoke of it as "Abraham's bosom" (in the parable of Dives and Lazarus), and "Paradise" (in his promise to the good Thief). Saint Peter calls it "prison" (1 Pet 3:19), theologians "Limbo", and in the English version of the Apostles' Creed it is called "hell".

5

THE INCARNATION

T HE HUMAN RACE then had broken its right relation of friendship with God: men had lost the way, because they had lost the Life, without which the way cannot be followed, and the truth, without which the way cannot even be known. To such a world Christ, who had come to make all things new, said, "I am the Way, the Truth and the Life." In those three words—way, truth, life—Christ related himself quite precisely to what man had lost: as precisely as a key fits a lock. In the precision of that threefold relation, we are apt to overlook the strangest word in the phrase—the word "am".

Men needed Truth and Life: what they might have expected was one who would say, "I have the Truth and the Life"; what they found was one who said, "I *am* the Truth and the Life." This strange word forces us to a new mode of approach. If a man claims to have what we want, we must study what he has. If a man claims to be what we want, we must study what he is. With any other teacher, the truth he has is our primary concern—the teacher himself is of no importance save as the bearer of truth, and his work is done when he has given it. With Christ, the teacher is primary: he cannot simply give us the Truth and the Life and then have done with us. He can only give us himself, for he is both. This point must be insisted on, not as a figure of speech, but as a strict fact. It is a map we are making, not a poem; and what is now being said, mysterious as it is, is strictly and literally true. Our study of the road of life has brought us to an examination of truth and life; we cannot understand the road if we do not understand them. But if Christ is the Truth, then we must understand him; if he is the Life, then *he* must live in us.

Obviously, then, our map-making cannot progress till we are clear about who and what Christ is, because the road we are to travel depends even more on what he is than on what he did.

The Two Natures of Christ

Christ is God-made-man: that is, he is truly God and he is truly man. He is God—with the nature of God; he took to himself and made his own a complete human nature—a real human body and a real human soul. He is, then, *one person*—God—with *two natures*—divine and human. Nor is all this mere abstract matter, of no real concern to us. Everything in our life is bound up with the one person and the two natures of Christ.

We must grasp this central luminous fact, or everything remains in darkness.

The distinction between person and nature is not some deep and hidden thing to which philosophy only comes after centuries of study. It is, on the contrary, a distinction so obvious that the smallest child who can talk at all makes it automatically. If in the half-light, he sees a vague outline that might be anything, he asks, "What is that?" If, on the other hand, he can see that it is a human being, but cannot distinguish or does not recognize the features, he asks, "Who is that?" The distinction between *what* and *who* is the distinction between *nature* and *person*. Of every man the two questions "What is he?" and "Who is he?" can be answered. Every man, in other words, is both a nature and a person. Into my every action, nature and person enter. For instance *I speak*. I, the person, speak. But I am able to speak only because I am a man, because it is of my nature to speak. I discover that there are all sorts of things I can do and all sorts of things I cannot do. My nature decides. I can think, speak, walk; these actions go with the nature of man, which I have. I cannot fly, for this goes with the nature of a bird, which I have not.

My nature, then, decides what I can do: it may be thought of as settling the sphere of action possible to me. According to my nature, I can act; apart from it, I cannot. But my nature does not do these things—I, the person, do them. It is not my nature that speaks, walks, thinks; it is I, the person.

A man may then be thought of as a person—who acts—and a nature—which decides the field in which he acts. In man, there is simply one nature to one person. In Christ, there are two natures to one person; and our minds, used to the one-nature-to-one-person state of man, tend to cry out that there is a contradiction in the idea of two natures to one person.

But once it has been grasped that "person" and "nature" are not identical in meaning; once it has been grasped that the person acts and the nature is that principle in him that decides his sphere of action, then we see that mysterious as our Lord's person and nature may be, there is no contradiction. God the Son, the second Person of the Blessed Trinity,[1] assumed—took to himself—a human nature: made it his own; not simply as something he could use as a convenient sphere to act in, but really as his own, just as our nature is our own. In us, the relation of person and nature is such that not merely do we say, "I *have* a human nature" (as we might say, "I have an umbrella") but person and nature are so fused in one concrete reality that we say "I am a man." So God the Son can say not only, "I am God with a human nature to act in", but in the most absolute fullness of meaning, he can also say, "I am man." He does not simply *act* as man; he *is* man —as truly man as we.

This *one* person has *two* spheres of action: Christ our Lord could act either in his nature as God or in his

---

[1] Something will be said of the doctrine of the Trinity in Chapter 8.

nature as man. Remember the principle stated a few
paragraphs back, that it is not the nature that acts, but
the person. Therefore, whether he was acting in his
divine nature or in his human nature, it was always the
person who acted; and there was only the one person
—God.

Then this is the position. Christ is God: therefore,
whatever Christ did, God did. When Christ acted in
his divine nature (as when he raised the dead to life)
it was God who did it; when Christ acted in his human nature (as when he was born, suffered, and died),
it was God who did it: God was born, God suffered,
God died. For it is the person who acts, and Christ is
God.

The Atonement

The next paragraph must be read with the closest attention or the map will not be properly understood.

Because Christ was God *and Man*, he was able to
effect the reconciliation of God and man. The human
race had broken the first relationship of oneness by sin,
and of itself, the human race with all its imperfections
on it could make no offering to God in reparation for
its sin. Literally, the human race *could not* make reparation. Yet for the human act of rebellion, a human
act of atonement was required: for the sin of human
nature, only an act of human nature could satisfy—
yet this act of human nature man could not perform.
Christ was God and Man. The acts he performed in

his human nature were truly human acts; yet because every action is of the person, they were acts of God, whose every act is of infinite value; thus Christ could make the necessary reparation. That particular action of his human nature that Christ chose as an offering in reparation—a sacrifice—was his death: at the age of thirty-three he was crucified upon Calvary.

This was the atonement. By it, the breach between God and the human race was closed. The race was redeemed from that condition of separation from God into which the sin of Adam, the representative man, had plunged it. Heaven, the final and eternal union of God and man, was once more possible to man. For even the holiest man of the time between Adam's fall and Christ's death was still a member of the human race, a member of the race that had lost oneness with God and as such was debarred from heaven. But, by this remaking of the oneness, not only was Life—the Supernatural Life—set flowing with new richness for the elevation of man's soul: but that Life could now in heaven receive the full and complete flowering that before Calvary was impossible to it.

Christ had come "to save his people from their sins": he had come that man "might have life and have it more abundantly." These two purposes are in reality the same purpose—the effect of sin is the destruction of the Supernatural Life: a soul in sin is a soul that lacks the Supernatural Life. Sin is removed by the pouring into the soul of that Life—as darkness is removed by the turning on of the light. So far, then, for the first part of Christ's mission: he had reconciled the human race to God; he had brought back the rich store of Supernatural Life.

Christ as Teacher

There remains to be considered the other need of man —Truth. As we have seen, this involves as a minimum that man shall be taught the purpose of his existence and the laws by which he must live. Christ taught this necessary minimum—and much more. The laws will be discussed in detail in Chapters 9 and 10; here notice only two things:

1. He took the ten commandments given to the Chosen People of Israel by God some fifteen hundred years before—most of them beginning with "Thou shalt not"—and summed them up into two, both beginning "Thou shalt". For the first three commandments, which set out our duty to God, he expressed concisely as "Thou shalt love God"; and the remaining seven, which set out our duty to our neighbour, he expressed equally concisely as "Thou shalt love thy neighbour." In other words, all the commandments lie implicit in this twofold love.

2. Just as the commandments are summarized and made positive, so they are traced back from external conduct to the internal root of conduct, from actions (commanded or prohibited) to love—a state of the soul. Sins of the mind—or heart—or intention become

as serious as sins of the exterior action: the yielding of the mind to lust not only is as bad as adultery, it *is* adultery; the yielding of the mind to murder not only is as bad as murder, it *is* murder. The essence of sin is now clear—it is the soul of man twisting itself out of the right relation to God. That is sin. Nothing else is. And the laws that express the right relation are all forms of *love*.

So much, for the moment, for the laws to be obeyed. On the truths to be believed—including the minimum requirement of the purpose of man's existence, of what was in the mind of God when he made man—Christ is equally revealing and equally fundamental. The purpose of man's existence is to come to God. This includes a multitude of things, but principally, because man is an intelligent being, it involves some revelation of the nature of God: the more man knows of his goal, the more likely he is to make for it effectively. Thus he revealed to man that in the divine nature are three persons—God the Father, God the Son, God the Holy Spirit—and that he himself was the second Person, God the Son. Of this supreme mystery of the Trinity and of mystery in general, something will be said in Chapter 8. Here we must consider not the revelation of God that our Lord gave by *teaching*, but the revelation of God that our Lord gave simply by *being*.

Mankind has never been without means of acquiring some knowledge of God: in the universe we have God's work before our eyes and by examining any work we can learn *something* of the workman. But, in practical fact, not much. We can learn more about a boilermaker by five minutes' face-to-face conversation with him than by five years' examination of the boiler he has made. Similarly, though we learn many things about God from contemplating the Universe He has made, there is something a little remote and shadowy about such knowledge. And this for the further reason that we can know nothing of what is involved in making a universe. But if we could see God —not making a universe—but obeying his mother, feeling hunger, paying taxes, receiving insult, then instantly we should be on our own ground. For all these things we have done ourselves. Now because Christ was God, all these things are there for men to see. God did obey his Mother, suffer hunger, pay taxes, receive insult. Christ, then, in a sense, is God translating himself into our nature. And the difference between God acting in his own nature and God acting in ours is as great as the difference between a man talking in his own language and the same man talking in ours. For in the first case, such a man can convey some things to us—but rather by signs than speech, and we catch what he has to say haltingly and uncertainly; in the second case, he really speaks to us, and we know what he wants to communicate.

Thus the fact that Christ is God takes on a new significance. As we first used it, it was as a fact about Christ; now we see it as an even more revealing fact about God. Christ acting in our nature, which he had made his, we can study and make our own; to realize that the knowledge thus acquired of Christ is true of God is altogether revolutionary. For only by learning that Christ is Love have men learned that God is Love; and that is almost the greatest gift of Christianity to the world.

Our Lord's life upon earth seems to have been especially devised with the purpose of bringing man into the closest possible intimacy with God. The general outline of his life is sufficiently well known. He was born of a virgin, the wife of a carpenter of Nazareth, during the reign of the Roman emperor Augustus. Then, with the exception of one strange incident when he was aged twelve, there is silence till he reached the age of thirty. Then came three years of teaching and the working of miracles. The leaders of the Jewish people turned against him and more or less forced the Roman governor to have him executed. He was nailed to a cross, and after three hours he died. On the third day, he rose again from the dead, and after forty days he ascended into the heavens and vanished from the eyes of men. Within this framework, there are two rich streams of human contact, a greater and a less. The greater, naturally enough, was through his Mother. From her he had drawn his human body; if man may call him brother, it is solely through her. She lived with him throughout the years before his public life began; to please her, he worked a miracle at Cana and began his public ministry sooner than he had meant. When he died, he committed her to the care of John, the follower he loved best: and this apostle, who became as a son to her, later wrote a gospel, in which from the beginning men have found a deeper insight into our Lord than in any other. It would have been strange had it been otherwise—if any man could have lived in such intimacy with the Mother of Christ and had no richness to show for it.

The second stream was through his apostles—the men he gathered round him and prepared with especial care as the instruments for the spread of his Kingdom among men. It is important to grasp here the mode of Christ's revelation of his own Godhead. Obviously, had he begun with the statement that he was God, the road would have been closed. Some would have disbelieved him; those who believed would have been far too overcome with terror at the majesty of God and their own sinfulness to make any progress in human intimacy with him. What actually happened was that these men came to know him as men can only know one in whose company they constantly are, in every variety of circumstance. Gradually—or rather with sudden bursts forward followed by fallings away —they came to the feeling that he *must* be God and ultimately to the full knowledge that he was. But before that time they had come to know him: to know him as a friend and not only as a master; from men who had companioned with Christ for three years, even the discovery that he was God could not take away the certainty that he was Love: so that God, too, must be Love. The fruit of our Lady's thirty years

with Christ and the apostles' three years with him, en-
shrined in part in the Gospels, is the very essence of the
Christian Tradition, woven into the very fabric of the
Christian mind.

If we compare the attitude to God of the most pi-
ous pagans with that of the Christian, the gulf is enormous. In the Christian attitude, there is a warm *personal* devotion not to be found elsewhere. For other
men have seen the works of God, but Christians have
seen God.

These two truths, *God is Love* and *Law is love*, are
the two specifically Christian truths, unknown outside
the Christian revelation. It is difficult to say which
idea would have come upon the world with a greater
shock. For outside Christianity, God has seemed to
be a master or even a tyrant, but never love; and as
a consequence, law has seemed to be force, or even
cruelty, but never love. And even inside Christianity,
it is hard to hold, continuous and never dimmed, the
idea of God and law as love: for there come moments
when another face seems to be presented to us; feeling
or no feeling, we know. And we know because Christ
was God.

Here then in outline is God's answer to man's need.
The human race needed first to be reunited to God
(that heaven might once more be open to it), and
second it needed the Life and the Truth by which
it might attain heaven once salvation became a possibility. Christ our Lord—God-made-man—made the

act of reparation that reunited the human race with God and so made heaven a possibility, brought back for man the rich profusion of the Supernatural Life, and revealed to man not only the necessary truths of purpose and law but a great store of truth besides. The next question is how man was to obtain what Christ had brought.

6

THE MYSTICAL BODY OF CHRIST

S O FAR WE HAVE SEEN that for the intelligent living of life, men need to know the purpose of their being and the laws by which they should govern their lives; and it has been established that man is totally incapable of finding these out for himself and can know them only if God reveals them. Further, we have seen that for the achievement of his purpose—namely, to live the life of heaven—the natural life of man is not sufficient: that men need certain further powers in the soul, that these flow from the Supernatural Life, that men must acquire this Supernatural Life here upon earth, and again that they cannot acquire it for themselves, but can have it only if God gives it.

These three things—Truth, Law, Life—we have seen, would have been necessary in any condition of the human race. But the first man—Adam—complicated the position by breaking the friendship of the human race with God and so closing heaven to the race. Heaven then had to be made once more a possibility, after which the three original requirements would still be in force. Christ came to offer himself as sacrifice to God in atonement for the sin of the race and so opened heaven once more to man; and he brought the gifts man needed of Truth, Law, and Life. On the question of how men were to obtain these gifts from him the last chapter closed.

Now to this question there is a very simple and satisfying answer. While he was upon this earth, Christ gathered a small band of followers, the disciples. Of these, he selected twelve—the apostles, of whom one, Peter, was singled out from the others—took them about with him, taught them, and when he was about to leave the earth gave them a commission to teach the truths and the laws he wished men to know and to administer the sacraments by which his life might flow to the souls of men. Thus, when he left the world, he left his followers as a body among whom were officials, with Peter at their head, who could transmit the Truth, Law, and Life men needed: by joining this body, then, men could receive from its officials what all men need. Christ extended their commission to all nations: that it might survive the ages, he extended it to the end of the world; that the teaching and the life might never fail, he promised to be with them in the work he had given them to do. Thus, then, you have his arrangement. His followers, still united with the successor of Peter, the visible point of unity, were to be one body till the end of time; and in that body they should receive teaching that is infallible, because Christ is with it, and sacraments that are channels of true life, because Christ is with them.

The Church, thus understood, is a great thing: a thing immeasurably beyond man's deserts, and fulfilling the three primary needs. But that is not all. He who sees only that is missing the depth of it.

For observe that, as stated, it leaves two questions unsettled. The first is this: the work of God among men is a close-knit, deeply intertwined thing without loose ends. Why then should men share in the benefits of Christ's atonement? He offered a redeeming sacrifice—but where do men come in? How can they share in his act?

And the second is this: Christ said: "I *am* the Way, the Truth, and the Life." The description of the Church set out above would be perfect if he had said *have*, but he said *am*. What has become of that mysterious word?

"I Am the Life"

Let us consider the second question first: Christ *is* the Life, the Life that must live in us if we are to be capable of heaven. *Christ then must live in us.* How? How can one being live in another? Here we must follow very closely. We dare not abandon the phrase with a vague feeling that its general meaning is obvious and edifying, but that it will not bear too close inspection. For he comes back to this idea of his living in men again and again, literally scores of times. Like every word of Christ, this one demands the closest scrutiny.

No words were ever weighed as his were, and if by chance we should forget that, Saint Paul shocks us back to attention: "I live, yet now not I, but *Christ liveth in me.*"

At the same time, our Lord constantly speaks of our living in him. There is then a twofold *in*. He must live in us. We must live in him.

In our own natures, we find the clue to the answer. Our bodies are composed of countless cells, living cells. The cells, we say, are living in the body. It would be truer to the order of real values to say that the body is living in the cells. That is the right order of thought. The cells live not with their own life, but with the life of the body. There is one life of the whole man, and by it the cells of his body live. Somehow then we must be in Christ as the cells are in our body: then Christ will live in us as we live in our bodily cells. Here again thought might falter; but Saint Paul works it out very clearly. Christ, living on this earth, had a human body, in which he worked among men. He taught with his lips, healed with his hands, converted sinners with the look of his eyes, gave Supernatural Life with his breath, made atonement with the suffering of his body. And all this, done through his body, was done by himself, God. He has left the earth; he is eternally in heaven at the right hand of the Father; but he still works among men in his body, no longer in his *natural body*, the body that was brought into being in the womb of Mary by the power of the Holy Spirit, but in his *Mystical* Body, the Church, the body that was brought into being in the Upper Room after his ascension by the power of the Holy Spirit. The Church, then, is his Body, linked to him really, organically, inseparably, as a body to its head: his life flows through the Church as my life flows through my body. My body has cells; and so has his. And as I live in the individual cells of *my* body, so he lives in the individual cells of his Body. Membership of his Church then means more than joining up with a useful organization from which many spiritual benefits may be derived. His Church is—mysteriously but *really*— his Body. Joining it means being built into his Body —that is to say, incorporated with him. Once we are thus incorporated with him, we are cells in his Body, he can live in us.

That is the Church—the living Body of Christ. Because of this, Christ could say to Saul when he was persecuting the Church—"Why persecutest thou Me?" So, Christ's own words "I am with you always even to the end of the world" have a more immense depth of meaning than we at first knew. So we see the meaning of that strange word *am*—"I am the Way, the Truth, and the Life." To be in the Way we must be in him; to possess the Truth we must possess him; to have the Life in us, he must live in us.

Redeemed Humanity

To this idea of the Church we have come, following up the second of the two questions left unsolved: it will now be seen that we have found the answer to the first as well—how can we share in Christ's atonement? It is easy enough to see how we are involved in Adam's loss: for Adam is the representative man, the ancestor of all men. In him, by nature, all men were incorporated. But men may be incorporated in Christ too, not by nature but by super-nature, not by birth but by baptism, the first of the sacraments (treated more fully in Chapter 11). That is the immense importance of baptism,[1] repeated again and again by Saint Paul: "Being baptized in Christ we have put on Christ." Incorporated with Adam by birth, which makes us men, we share in his loss: incorporated with Christ by baptism, which makes us Christians, we share in his act of redemption. Both Adam and Christ are representative men: Adam because he is the first man, Christ because he is the perfect man. Adam was the head of the human race; Christ is the head of redeemed humanity. We come from Adam; we come to Christ.

In this view of the Church, we see how all our needs are met. Incorporated, built into the Mystical Body of Christ, we share in the benefits of his atonement, we are reconciled with God, and to us, as members of redeemed humanity, heaven is once more open. From that Church, which is thus united with Christ, we receive Christ's teaching—so that we may know the truths bearing on the meaning and purpose of our

[1] This book is concerned with God's plan for mankind in what may be called its normal working. There is no discussion here of the position of those who are not baptized or of baptized non-Catholics.

lives, and the laws by which we may live rightly. In that Church, we are so united to Christ that the Supernatural Life pours into our souls. The whole of man's needs are thus met, those needs that have been kept constantly in mind from the beginning of this book.

But there is a wider horizon yet. This Mystical Body of Christ is the Church. But the Church is not only a thing of this world. It contains not only its members still in this life, but also all who have died with the Supernatural Life in their souls—whether, having attained their goal, they are in heaven or, in final preparation for heaven, they are in Purgatory.

The Mystical Body is a growing body. All who die with the Supernatural Life are in it for ever: each new member is a new cell. There will come a point, Saint Paul tells us, when the Mystical Body will have grown to its perfect stature, in some such way as a natural body reaches its fullest development. When that time comes, the human race will have achieved its purpose and the world will come to an end. For there is a purpose for the whole race as well as for the individual man, and the end of the world will be not simply a decision by God that the world has gone on long enough, but will definitely mean that the race has achieved its purpose.

But the end of the world is not yet. And meanwhile the Church is in the world, acting upon her members, acting upon the world at large. Not all her members here below are fully receptive of the life of Christ:

some, as we shall see in a moment, while remaining members, have totally shut off from their souls the stream of Christ's life. Thus the Church, the actual visible Church here below, presents herself under a double aspect. Insofar as it is Christ himself living in men—for the teaching of truth, for the promulgation of the moral law, for the lifegiving work of the sacraments—she is perfect. Insofar as she is considered in her human members (even her officials) vivified in their varying degrees or not vivified at all by the life of the Body, she is always short of perfection, sometimes very far short. But perfect she is one day to be.

The Communion of Saints

Meanwhile see how the map of life grows in the light of this fact of the Church. We have to live our lives not as isolated units, but as members of a living thing, united organically with Christ and with all men, living and dead, who are in the love of God. This is the full force of the communion of saints—the oneness of all men in Christ.

Because we are members of Christ's Body, we are one with him; and also we are one with one another. In a body, one member can help another: if the foot be hurt, the hand can tend it. So in the Mystical Body: one man can help another, by prayer and teaching and sacrifice. Here upon earth our prayers for one another are thus fruitful; we can pray for the souls in Purgatory; the souls in heaven can pray for us. It has to

some been a difficulty that death should be no barrier to this stream of prayer. That one living Christian
should pray for another, or ask another to pray for
him, has always seemed obviously right. But within
the Body of Christ, death makes no difference. The
soul of one who has left this world is not less a member of the same Body as we, but is living more in-
tensely with the life of Christ that we also share. If we
should have asked him to pray for us during his life,
we do so now more than ever. One striking charac-
teristic of the Catholic Church is that real friendships
do exist between her children still upon earth and one
or other of the saints in heaven. Sin is a barrier between souls; death is not. There is this constant flow
of prayer throughout the whole body; for we are not
members simply of one society, we are members of
one thing—a living thing.

Life in the Body

It is necessary now to see what all this comes to in
practical effect upon us. We are cells in the Body of
Christ, so that he lives in us and we have one life in
common with all men, in this world and the next, who
are in the love of God. But observe that all this refers
to the *Supernatural* Life—the life by which man is to
be able to live the life of heaven. *Supernaturally*, we,
the cells, live with the life of Christ. But our natural
life is not destroyed; and *naturally* we live with our
own lives. Now it is part of our nature that we have

free will, and part of our natural life to exercise it. We can do so in one of three ways: we can yield our wills wholly to God; or we can yield them to God, but not wholly; or we can reject God. And according to the use we thus make will be our state in the Mystical Body. If we yield ourselves wholly to the Supernatural Life, the life of the Mystical Body, then we are living supernaturally at the fullest intensity. If our wills are not *wholly* yielded to God, then we hinder the flow of the Supernatural Life in us, and though we are living supernaturally, though we are still sharing the life of the Body so that Christ really lives in us, yet that life is not present in its fullest intensity.

And if, being once incorporated—that is, built into the Body of Christ—our wills turn against God and reject him for self, then we shut off the stream of life altogether, and though we remain in the Body, we are dead cells[2]—retaining our natural life, which is of no avail for salvation—but without the Supernatural Life. While we are still in this world, Supernatural Life may be set flowing again, as we shall see. But if at the moment of our earthly death we are thus dead cells in the Body, we are cut out from the Body and eternally lost.

Sufficient has been said to show how our position in the Church lays open to us Life and the knowledge of

[2] For a more detailed discussion of the state of those who have lost the Supernatural Life, see p. 129

Truth and Law. It remains now to examine the Truth, the Law, and the Life in detail. Two chapters will be devoted to each of these.

7

TRUTH: THE TEACHING CHURCH

WE HAVE SEEN THAT MAN, by membership in Christ's Church, receives the three things necessary—Truth, Law, Life. The next step is to examine each of these three in more detail. This chapter and the next will be concerned with Truth.

Christ gave to his Church, in the person of its first officials, the apostles, a mass of truth concerning God and man: concerning the nature of God, his threefold personality, his attributes, his purpose in making man, the means by which his purpose was to be achieved. This teaching, given by Christ to the apostles, was by them passed on to others, who in their turn passed it on. Some of it was, by the inspiration of God, written down. The part written down, what we now call the New Testament, was small in relation to the whole mass of teaching, but of priceless value.

The Scriptures

In thus inspiring men to write, God was continuing in the Church what he had begun with his Chosen People.

This fact of inspiration marks off certain books from all other writings in the world. It involves a special relation of God to the human author and to the thing written, not to be found elsewhere. God so acted upon the mind and will of the author that what was written was what God wanted written. The inspired writing of the Jews—collected together in the Old Testament—were in sum a record of the creation and fall of man, God's dealing with fallen humanity, and the preparation for the coming of a Saviour. The New Testament shows the Saviour actually in the world, doing the work he came to do, and arranging for its continuation to the end of time. It falls roughly into three divisions: (1) the four Gospels (already touched upon in Chapter 5) are records of Christ's life upon earth; (2) the Acts of the Apostles and a handful of letters—written mainly by Saint Paul—show the Church facing her first disciplinary and doctrinal problems; (3) Revelation is a series of visions concerned mainly with the universal conflict of good and evil and its ultimate issue.

Development of Doctrine

The Church then, by the time the last apostle died, had all the mass of truth the apostles had taught, the whole of it by word of mouth, a part of it in writing. She might have simply gone on, through the nineteen centuries since, repeating what had been taught, reading what had been written. In this case, she would have been a preserver of truth—but scarcely a teacher.

She would have been a piece of human machinery, but not a living thing, not the Mystical Body of Christ. In fact, she not only repeated what the apostles had been taught: she thought about it, meditated on it, prayed by it, lived it. And, doing all this, the Church came to see further and further depths of truth in it. And, seeing these, she taught these too. Everything was contained in what Christ had given the apostles to give the Church: but though everything was there, it was not all seen explicitly—not all at once. A rough comparison may make the position clear: a man brought into a dark room begins by distinguishing little; then he sees certain patches of shadow blacker than the rest; bit by bit he sees these as a table and chairs; then, as his eyes grow accustomed to the obscurity, he sees things smaller still—pictures, books, ash trays—and so on to the smallest detail. Nothing has been added to the contents of the room; but there has been an immense growth in his knowledge of the contents. So with the Church. She has, generation by generation, seen deeper and deeper. This development in the Church's understanding of what has been committed to her is not like anything else in the world. Science, for instance, progresses, but its progress consists to a large extent in discovering and discarding its own errors. The teaching of the Church develops by seeing further truths. At every stage, the Church adds something, but not at the cost of discarding anything. At every stage, all she teaches is true; at no stage does she teach all that is contained in the Truth.

This development—which we find in theology and nowhere else—combines two things: the work of men's minds and the overruling protection of God. In theology, as in science, progress comes by the minds of men working on what they have been taught: but left to themselves, men may simply make further mistakes. In science, they do so. In the teaching of the Church, they do not; and the reason is that God intervenes, to prevent the teaching of error by his Church. God's actions—whether revelation or sacrament or miracle— are never labour-saving devices: God does not do them to save men the trouble of doing what they can very well do for themselves. In revelation, for instance, God teaches men what they could not (at any rate, could not with absolute sureness) find out for themselves; but having given them that, he leaves it to them to meditate upon it and arrive at a clearer understanding of it. He does not do their thinking for them.

The Teaching Church

But if we are to say that in the teaching of the Church there are no mistakes, it is necessary to look a little more closely at what we mean by the phrase "the Teaching Church". The first teachers in the Church were the apostles; their successors are the bishops. The bishops are the teaching body of the Church. Therefore, since God will not have his Church taught error as to his doctrine, he will not allow the bishops to teach error. This or that bishop or group of bishops may give wrong teaching in theology. But what is taught by the bishops as a body cannot be wrong. On some given subject, it might be difficult to know what the bishops as a body do teach: in that case, they might be gathered together in a General Council where they could state their teaching and so place it beyond doubt. But however we come by the knowledge, once we do know what the bishops as a body teach, we know the certain truth, for their teaching is guaranteed by God. And that is the ordinary way in which the Catholic does learn God's truth—from the teachers appointed by his bishop. But there is another way—an extraordinary way. The bishops as a body are not allowed by God to teach what is wrong on matters of faith or morals revealed by him: this is what we mean when we say they are infallible. But one of them, the head, Christ's representative on earth, the bishop of Rome, whom we call the Pope, is infallible,[1] independently of the other bishops. And in case of doubt as to what

[1] This book is concerned with Catholic doctrine from a special point of view, the view of a map-maker. Infallibility, therefore, is treated only as it bears upon the Catholic's need to learn the truth. It may be useful to consider it for a moment in its effect upon the man who has it. It has no necessary effect at all. His infallibility exists, not for his own sake, but for ours. It is of no more benefit to him than it is to us. It does not make virtue easier for him or sin less attractive. It does not, therefore, make the salvation of his soul any easier. It is simply a way in which God uses him for the preservation of truth. And as it does not affect his character, so it does not arise from it. If by chance a bad man is Pope, it is just as necessary for us that he should be prevented from teaching error and just as easy for God to prevent him!

bishops teach, a definition by the Pope himself is sufficient to inform us of the truth.

But if the body of bishops, with the Pope at their head, are the sole infallible teachers of doctrine, they are not the only people in the Church who are studying doctrine. Every Catholic does it to some extent; theologians give their lives to it. Throughout the ages, there has never ceased to be a stream of solid thinking on theology. Now this thinking is the thinking of men: the result of their thinking may be the emergence of some truth not previously so clearly seen; but likewise the result of their thinking may be error. How shall men know which it is? It is for the bishops to decide. If it is true, then they adopt it and teach it. If it is false, God does not allow them to adopt it and teach it. An erroneous view might become current, even widely current. Sooner or later the teaching authority acts and the erroneous view is declared to be erroneous. A theologian who has fallen into error may persist in his error—become a heretic. The very task of refuting him leads to a closer examination and thus to a better understanding of the doctrine at issue.

But the decision of the bishops as a body—or of the bishop of Rome as head—is final. And that, as we have seen, is watched by God: he does not allow them to teach his Church what is wrong. He does not add new teaching or fill their minds with new doctrine: for that they must use their minds in the ordinary way of man. But he prevents falsehood from being *taught* by them.

To put this matter in a nutshell. The ordinary man has three courses open to him—he may say what is right, he may say what is wrong, or he may be silent. The infallible man has only two. He is prevented by God from saying what is wrong. He may therefore say what is right, or he may be silent. As to which of these alternatives he shall pursue in a particular case, what is he to decide? As between teaching what is right and remaining silent, his infallibility will not help. It prevents him from teaching what is wrong. It can do no more for him. What, then, is to decide whether he shall teach right or remain silent? He can say what is right only if he knows what is right—if, that is, he has made the fullest possible use of all the means of acquiring knowledge. If he does not know the right answer, he must remain silent: and this might very well happen. A Pope does not necessarily by some miracle know the whole of Catholic doctrine, the answer to every doctrinal question that could be raised. The Church, of course, is ruled over by the providence of God, and if some teaching were at a given moment essential for the Church's well-being, God would see that we had it. But I am concerned here with the human machinery, so to speak, of infallibility. And it remains true that what he does not know he cannot teach. But in no case can he teach what is wrong: for God will not let him, lest we, the members of the Church, be led into error.

One further thing remains to be said. We believe what the Church teaches because the Church is the Mystical Body of Christ, because, therefore, her teaching is the voice of Christ himself. Among the mass of the things she teaches and the moral laws she propounds, some are, as it were, easy for the human mind, some difficult. For some we seem to see a score of reasons, for some we see no reason at all, some actually might seem to us against reason. But all alike we accept on the one secure ground—that the Church teaches them. We do not accept the easy ones because we can see why, and the others only by an act of faith. We accept the easy ones—because the Church teaches them; and we accept the difficult ones—because the Church teaches them. When a doctrine or a moral law is presented to us we may ask what are the reasons for it, but only that we may the better comprehend it, not that we may decide whether or not to obey it. For that we only ask if the Church teaches it. For it is thus that Christ would have us know the truths by which our lives are to be lived.

8

TRUTH: THE MYSTERY
OF THE TRINITY

THUS THEN WE ARE in a position to learn from the Church the truths Christ entrusted to her, and these truths cover not only the bare minimum of necessary things—purpose and law—but also much besides for the further enrichment of man's mind and man's life. All that is set forth in these articles is simply the general outline of it. It contains the great mysteries of the Trinity, creation, grace, redemption, the Mystical Body, the sacraments, hell, and heaven. Some of these have already been looked at, at least in part: the others will be looked at in later chapters. Here I wish to speak only of mystery in general and of the greatest of all mysteries, the Trinity.

Mystery

First of mystery. As used by theologians, the word does not mean a truth of which we cannot know anything: it means a truth of which we cannot know everything. Mystery there *must* be once we touch the nature of God. He is the Infinite, the Immeasurable, the Limitless. We are finite, measured, limited on all sides. It is impossible that we should totally contain God in our minds so as totally to comprehend him. But by his loving kindness we are endowed with a nature that can know something of him—some little by its own powers, vastly more by what he tells us of himself in the mysteries he has revealed.

But a mystery is not merely a truth about God that we cannot discover for ourselves and can know only if God reveals it. If it were only that, the subject would present no difficulties. There is the further fact already suggested: that, even when God has revealed it to us, it remains a truth about an infinite being and is therefore not fully comprehensible by us. And the trouble is that it first presents itself to the mind as an apparent contradiction in terms. Thus the mystery of the Trinity appears as a statement that there are three Persons, each of them God, yet not three Gods. Transubstantiation appears as a statement that what, by every test known to man, is bread is yet the Body of Christ. And so with the others. Now contradiction is the enemy of thought. If any article of belief presented for the mind's acceptance appears to contain a contradiction within itself, then the mind cannot be at ease with it. So that a mystery of religion presents itself first to the mind rather as a burden than as a light.

Now in some cases, the sense of contradiction arises

from a sheer misunderstanding of the doctrine and can be removed instantly by a correct statement. But in others it arises from a defect in the mind—the defect of superficiality.

Two statements appear to be at variance. The mind scrutinizes them more closely and still cannot see how they are to be reconciled. Now the fact that the mind cannot reconcile the two statements may originate either in the statements or in the mind: either the statements may be in fact irreconcilable, or the reconciliation may be at a depth to which the mind cannot pierce. This double possibility will always be obvious to a mind that has realized the surface of a thing is not the whole of it.

For the mind to proceed from the affirmation that it cannot reconcile two statements to the affirmation that they are in contradiction is legitimate only on one condition: that both are fully understood. If two statements are fully comprehended and yet cannot be reconciled, then there is real contradiction and one of them must be false. But in these mysteries of religion, it soon becomes clear that the truths concerned plunge rapidly into depths where the mind cannot follow them. It still cannot see how they are to be reconciled: but realizing how immeasurably more there is in them than it can comprehend, will not assume that one of them must be false.

The result is that though it may still find them irreconcilable, this ceases to be a burden to it. The sense of contradiction, the one burden the mind finds intolerable, has vanished. The discovery of its own limitation does not thus trouble it. And the discovery that there are depths beyond depths of truth is the strongest possible stimulus to the mind.

For to call a doctrine a mystery is not to warn men's minds off it, as though it were something on which thought cannot profitably be employed. It is not to be conceived as a blank wall barring further progress; it is to be thought of rather as an endless gallery, into which we can advance ever deeper, to the great enrichment of our minds, but to the end of which we shall never come. Or better still, think of it as an inexhaustible well of truth—a well from which for all eternity we can drink our fill yet which in all eternity we shall never drink to the last drop—so that we shall never know thirst. This infiniteness of truth is the most splendid assurance we can have of eternal happiness, for it means that the mind can progress forever, that it will forever be enriched by new draughts of truth, yet it will never reach the end of truth. This inexhaustibility of truth is our guarantee against stagnation of the mind: it guarantees to our minds the possibility of progress through all eternity.

Mystery then is not the prohibition of thinking, but actually an invitation to think. The mysteries revealed by God are revealed as food for the mind, not as dangerous things that should be left alone. Every mystery contains a central nucleus of truth that is comprehended, surrounded on all sides by things that we do not comprehend. Think of it as a globe of light surrounded by darkness. The man who rejects mystery is rejecting the central globe of light and accepting the impenetrable darkness. Whereas for the man who accepts it, the light grows and expands, sending longer and longer rays into the darkness around.

The Doctrine of the Trinity

Thus the doctrine of the Trinity, at first seen only as a sheer challenge to faith, grows steadily more luminous to the mind that accepts it and comes humbly to the study of what the Church has seen in it. This truth that the Godhead is absolutely one essence, one single concrete Something, yet that there are three Persons owning the *one* nature—the one self-same identical nature, this truth not only grows more luminous as the ideas of person and nature are studied, as the relation of Father and Son and the Spirit proceeding from both is meditated on, but throws a flood of light on the whole of our understanding of life.

The doctrine that in the unity of the Godhead there are three Persons truly distinct is the supreme mystery revealed by Christ. Beyond it is no further mystery, for it deals with the innermost life of God. In a sense, man need never have been taught it apart from the Incarnation: for it is God in his unity who acts in relation to created beings, the threefold personality being a fact of his own inner life, of his own internal activity, of that activity that remains within his own nature and does not directly affect the beings he has created. But it is a property of love that it wants not only to know but also to be known by the person loved. God, loving us, wants us to know him in his deepest and most secret life, and so gives us here upon earth a glimpse of that truth that it is man's proper destiny to spend eternity in contemplating. And, apart from that desire of God's to be known by man, the distinction of Persons has in fact a direct bearing on man's life since it was the Second Person, and not God in his threefold personality, who became man for our salvation.

It is the supreme mystery in a double sense: it deals with the highest truth, and it is most inaccessible to the created mind. Yet certain elements of it can be grasped by us.

In the first place, it states that in the one divine nature there are three Persons. The distinction between nature and person has already been discussed in Chapter 5, and the reader might very well return to it before proceeding here. Summarizing what is there said: nature and person are both principles of action but in different senses—the person being that which acts, the nature being that by which he acts. In man, nature and person coalesce in one concrete living being: but the attempt to analyse these two principles that in us are fused into one has two results: (1) it makes clear that we are far from reaching down into the depths of either principle: their deepest depths escape us and it would be a bold man who would dogmatise as to their uttermost possibilities; (2) it at least suggests to us that the total expression of one nature in one person, which is in us, is not the only possibility. Person may be seen as the "centre of attribution in a rational nature"—that to which the actions of a rational nature are attributed. In an infinite nature, might there not be more than one such centre of attribution? Is the idea of one single mind and one single will three times focused totally self-contradictory?

No one dare affirm that there is any such contradiction. The mind of man may say, "I cannot see the possibility"; it dare not say, "I see the contradiction." To the mind thus faltering comes the revelation of God that it is so, and contained within the revelation are certain truths that help the mind to progress in it. God has not simply revealed to us a handful of words.

The three Persons—the Father, the Son, the Holy Spirit—each possess the one divine nature: they do not share it: they each possess it in its totality. It is important to grasp exactly what this means. Men, we say, have one nature, in the sense that they all are human, and human nature is one thing. But though Brown and I are of one nature, I cannot think with Brown's mind nor love with Brown's will. I must think with my own mind and love with my own will. So that, although in a general sense human nature is one, in the concrete, each man has his own nature and acts in it. With the three Persons of the Trinity this is not so. There is but one divine nature, one divine mind, one divine will. The three Persons each use the one mind to know with, the one will to love with. For there is but the one absolute divine nature. Thus there are not three

Gods, but one God. The Christian revelation cannot allow the faintest derogation from pure monotheism. The three Persons, then, are not separate. But they are distinct. The Father is God, the Son is God, the Holy Spirit is God. But the Father is not the Son, nor the Son the Holy Spirit, nor the Holy Spirit the Father.

What distinction can there be in three Persons who each possess the totality of one and the same nature? A distinction of relations.[1]

What then are these relations?

For the relation between the first and second Persons, the Gospels use two terms. The second Person is the Son; and he is the Word. Both, by different approaches, bring us to the same Truth.

A son proceeds from his father by generation. One of the enormous difficulties in all discussion about God is that we are forced to use human language. Having been built up by the mind of man for the expression of man's experience, human language is necessarily inadequate for the expression of the divine. Yet it is the best we have. No higher is within our power. And provided the inadequacy is remembered, there is no harm done. But, in addition to the sheer inadequacy of speech, for which there is no remedy, there is another way in which language can mislead, and this can be remedied by taking thought. Ideas that are in themselves quite simple get tied up in our minds with other ideas, because in human experience the two things are

[1] These relations, as we shall see, are subsistent and not, as relations are in created beings, mere accidents.

always found together. Thus the moment we think of the words "father" and "son", we think of the father as older than the son, as existing before the son. But in applying words to the understanding of God, we must get at the essence of the word and take away from it whatever ideas belong merely to the condition of human life.

The relation of "paternity" in the Godhead is not modelled upon human paternity; on the contrary, human paternity is a shadow of the absolute fatherhood of the first Person of the Trinity. Thus a very slight examination of the idea of generation as such shows that the time element does not belong to it. Generation means simply the origin of a living thing from another living thing, by communication of substance, *unto similitude of nature*. Wherever in the origin of a being these two conditions are fulfilled—communication of substance, similitude of nature—then there is sonship. The time element proceeds not from the nature of sonship, but from the finite nature of man: he must reach a certain point of development before he can generate a son. But in an infinite being, to whom time is not, there is no such requirement. God the Father eternally generates God the Son, who is thus coeternal and, as a consequence of likeness in nature where the nature is infinite, coequal.

The term word—the word of the mind, which is thought—brings us to the same truth and in a way to a greater point of understanding. The first Person, as thinker, thinks. Now that which is produced by the

act of thinking, what we call the "term" of the act,
is a thought. With men, the thought is more or less
adequate to the object they are thinking about. But
with God, whose intelligence is infinite, the thought
is absolutely adequate to the object. In this instance,
God's thought is of himself, and since it is absolutely
adequate, it is the perfect image of himself, and so
living, coeternal, equal in all perfections: a Person.
Thus, even more clearly than sonship, this notion of
the Word shows the second Person as the perfect image of the first, shows also how there is no new nature
produced, for there is no more complete oneness of
nature than that which exists between the Thinker and
the Thought.

Thus we have the first Person and the second proceeding from the first by way of generation. But between Father and Son (or between Thinker and
Thought) there is Love. Here we must proceed with
the greatest care. In our human experience, the term of
an act of thinking is a thought, something that remains
within the being of the thinker; and it is this thought
and not the act of thinking that we conceive as the second Person. Can we say that love likewise produces
a "term" within the lover? Saint Thomas tells us that
we can. Though love tends toward a being outside itself, yet the act of loving arouses a state of warmth in
the soul by which the being that is loved is present to
the affections. This state is not the act of loving, but
is produced in the soul by the act of loving, is what
we have called a "term" of the act. And so it is in

the love with which God loves himself—that is, with which the Father loves the Son and the Son the Father. The "term" of that act of love (like the earlier term of the act of thinking) is subsistent, is a Person—the third Person of the Blessed Trinity, the Holy Spirit.

On this matter of the "procession"[2] of the Holy Spirit as breathed forth by God in an act of love, we cannot claim revelation. It is Saint Augustine's magnificent contribution to the theology of that which we do know by revelation—that the Holy Spirit is the third Person of the Trinity, coeternal and coequal with the Father and the Son.

I have said that God acts upon creatures in his unity, rather than in his Trinity. Yet we have his own warrant for associating certain of these actions with one or other of the three Persons. The Father we say creates, the Son redeems, the Holy Spirit sanctifies. The principle of this "appropriation" is quite clear: the external operations of God can be particularly attributed

[2] The act by which the Holy Spirit subsists is not "generation" —this we know by revelation, God the Son is "the only begotten of the Father". The Holy Spirit, says the Athanasian Creed is "from the Father and the Son, neither made, nor created, nor begotten, but proceeding". What is the difference between the generation of the Son and the "spiration" or breathing forth of the Holy Spirit? Many answers are suggested. Saint Thomas finds the difference in this: an act of the intellect has as its precise object the production of a term in the likeness of the thing conceived, and likeness is an essential of sonship; whereas though the Holy Spirit is in fact like in nature to the Father and Son, yet likeness is not the primary object of an act of the will.

to one Divine Person rather than another if they are especially bound up with the relation of that Person within the Godhead; that is, the Persons may be spoken of as having relations to mankind similar to their relations within the Godhead. Thus, because the Son is brought forth by an act of the divine intellect, the works of wisdom are especially attributed to him. Because the Holy Spirit proceeds from the divine will, the works of holiness are attributed to him (since holiness is of the will as wisdom is of the intellect) and so also are God's gifts to men (since the Holy Spirit is Love, and gifts are the expression of love). The operation of the Holy Spirit within the Mystical Body will be treated later.

In thus setting down some of the elements of what God has revealed to us of his own innermost life, it is clear that the mystery remains, but it is mystery in the sense indicated earlier in this chapter—the reconciliation remains invisible to us, but it is rather the invisibility that comes from too much light than from sheer darkness. Thus it is an invitation to the mind. Already, the mind is freed by it from the awful weight of God conceived as solitary in infinity, with no adequate object of his infinite love. And new richness comes into our contemplation of human nature: thus human fatherhood is an immeasurably greater thing as a shadow of the divine fatherhood than it could ever be in its own right: the human soul is only the more like to God for its faculties of intellect and will, since in God Thought and Love not only exist, but subsist as Persons; and the unity of the Church takes on a new immensity when Christ proposes as its model the unity of the Triune God.

9

LAW AND SIN

C HRIST SUMMARIZED the duty of man in the two phrases: "Love God" and "love thy neighbour as thyself." We cannot have the Supernatural Life if we do not love God and our neighbour. But love must express itself in act, and our Lord left us not only the summarization, but also a great body of detailed rules concerning things to be done as an expression of the twofold love and things to be avoided as contrary to it. These, then, are the laws established by God for the guidance of man's actions. The means by which men can learn what the laws are, and certain practical problems to which they give rise, will be examined in the next two chapters.

Conscience

Now many will think that this is precisely what conscience is for. And it is absolutely true that a man must in all circumstances follow his conscience. But an investigation of conscience will show that by itself it is not sufficient—that man has not within himself an infallible teacher as to what is right and what is wrong. Conscience is not a faculty or permanent part of man. It is loose speaking to say "I have something on my conscience." It would be more accurate to say "I have something on my soul." There is the same difference between conscience and soul as there is between a punch and a fist. The punch is an action of the fist, a thing the fist does. Similarly the conscience is an action of the soul, a thing the soul does. Precisely defined, conscience is the practical moral judgment of the intellect—the intellect being simply the soul itself considered in its activity of knowing things.

Whenever I am asked a question, the answer is a judgment of my intellect. Now the intellect makes many judgments, and conscience only differs from the others by its special scope. If I answer the question "Did Richard III murder the princes in the Tower?" my answer is a judgment of my intellect; but it is purely a historical judgment, not a moral one; therefore it is not my conscience. If the question is changed to "Ought Richard III to have murdered the princes?" my answer is again a judgment of my intellect, and this time it is a moral judgment, a judgment on right and wrong. But it is not my conscience, for it is not a *practical* moral judgment, that is to say it is not concerned with what it would be right for me to do here and now. But if the question is again changed to "Ought I to murder the man next door whose manners are so maddening?" the answer is not only a judgment of my intellect and a moral one, but also a practical one.

In other words, conscience is the answer given by my soul when I am faced with the question "What ought I to do, what would it be right for me to do, in this particular matter?"

Yet, you say, is that not a sufficient guide? Unfortunately no. For conscience is a judgment of my intellect and therefore like any other such judgment it can be wrong. Conscience is not universally infallible. It is often firm and definite in its answer; but an answer may be firm and definite, and yet wrong. By what does the soul judge, if it has no teacher outside itself? By what standard does it decide what is right? The answer is that the law of God is imprinted on man's nature and by that he judges. In other words, God's laws for men are not something totally outside his nature: they correspond to something God has already placed *in* his nature. But in the course of ages, man's nature has grown distorted in all sorts of ways and any distortion in man's nature will mean a distortion in the thing imprinted on it. The moon, falling on a perfectly still lake, will give a perfect image of itself; but let the lake be ever so slightly ruffled, and the image will be broken up into small pieces; let the lake be really ruffled, and the image will be no more than broken sparkles of light scattered here and there. It is still from the moon that these sparkles come, but no one looking at them could form a picture of the lovely luminous globe of the moon itself. Thus, even where the distortion is greatest, no man's nature is without some trace of God's law still imprinted; but it is not always easy to read. If we could take the general consensus of the conscience of the race as a whole, it would probably be found to be in accord with the greater part of the natural moral law. But the individual conscience, though probably also in major accord, is apt to show startling variations, from country to country and from man to man.

Thus, even on matters that simply concern the right use of man's *nature*, conscience—lacking information from without—can give contradictory answers. But on the most important questions of all—those concerned with man's supernatural destiny—the unaided conscience gives no answer at all. On the question "Ought I to divorce my wife?" conscience, apart from God's teaching, gives different men different answers. But on the question "Ought I to be baptized?" conscience, apart from God's teaching, gives no man any answer.

If, then, there is no teacher capable of giving us God's law, we are left with nothing but this internal judgment of our own, which on the most obvious questions is *capable* of being wrong and on the most important questions can only be silent. A man *must* follow his conscience, the judgment of his intellect as to what is right and wrong. But the very supremacy of conscience renders it vital that conscience should be instructed.

Consider man's position. There is in him no internal

faculty that tells him with either certainty or completeness, in every situation that can arise, what things are right and what wrong. Yet without such knowledge how can he so act as to reach his goal? The task of achieving the end for which one is created is like any other task: it must be done in the right way. Certain actions will help the achievement, certain will hinder it. We can only know if we are told. God who made us has told us: his Church, which enunciates his truths, likewise enunciates his laws. Nor is conscience thereby annulled: conscience is the practical moral judgment of the intellect. Now the intellect that knows that the Church is giving God's law will naturally judge that it is right. The Catholic who unquestioningly accepts the moral law as taught by the Church is following his conscience unswervingly.

Sin

The Catholic therefore knows the law of right action. But knowledge is not enough. A man may know and yet disobey. Such disobedience is sin. Sin is, quite simply, breaking God's law. And in that lies its enormity.

The breach of God's law may be a small thing or a great. It may be a failing in a comparative trifle—silly and weakening to the soul; or it may be a definite rejection of God. The first sort—venial sin—is still sin, yet it will not break the friendship that exists between the soul and God: it will not therefore damn a man's soul. The second sort we call mortal: having committed such a sin, to die without repentance means eternal damnation.[1] We shall return to that.

The essence of sin's gravity, as I have said, lies simply in its breaking of God's law. It is blank ingratitude to God; to whom all men owe so much—to whom Christians know that they owe so immeasurably more than the rest of man.

It is incredible stupidity: rebellion against God is one of the most ludicrous things in the world. For whether we are obedient or rebellious we are at every moment totally in the hands of God. He made us of nothing; by his almighty power he keeps us above the surface of our native nothingness. Without his concurrence, we could not act at all, we could not even defy him. The sinner, as it were, stands up in the hand of God, sustained in being by that all-powerful hand, defying God, but in his very defiance using the power God has lent him and that God could at any moment withdraw from him.

---

[1] The distinction between mortal and venial sin is very important. Between two breaches of law there may not only be a difference of degree, but actually a difference of kind. Consider the law of the land. A man may break it by not taking out a dog licence. Or he may break it by fighting against his country in war. It is not simply that one breach of the law is more serious than the other. The two breaches are totally different in their nature. So with the law of God. There are breaches of his law that do not involve rejection and rebellion, others that do.

This fact that the essence of sin is offence against the law of God sometimes—in fact most often—misleads the sinner as to the true nature of sin. He imagines himself in a small field, bounded by a fence put there to prevent him from breaking out of the field to sample the rich possibilities of life outside. Here, he says, am I: a being full of the possibilities of development, yet my development is checked at every turn by some absurd law. This view arises from a failure to understand the nature of God's laws. His laws are no mere whims, like the laws of some stupid despot. They are, on the contrary, the expression by God of his own knowledge of man's nature and destiny. He knows the kind of being man is, for he made him. And for the same reason he knows what man is made for. God's laws, then, are a precise statement of how this particular kind of being may avoid destruction and reach his particular goal. The man who makes an engine is not limiting your freedom when he tells you not to run it beyond a certain speed. He knows that if you do you will smash the engine. And if you should plead that your nature demands more speed, that you feel stifled by such slow running—he may very well grow impatient. He knows what speed is right for the engine, for he made it.

God's laws then are best thought of as "maker's instructions", directions for the right use of ourselves. His prohibitions warn us of wrong ways of using our-

selves or our neighbours. Earlier I used the simile of a
razor to illustrate the point that to misuse a thing was
to destroy it. Emancipate the razor from its old hum-
drum task of removing hair from the face—defy the
maker's statement that razors are only meant for shav-
ing—use your razor for chopping wood and you will
have a piece of twisted metal, fit only for the scrap-
heap. God's law is not something altogether apart from
us: the knowledge of it may have to come from outside, but the law itself is, in a special sense, inside us.
For it is a statement of the way we are made. And any
action against it is therefore an action against our own
nature and is consequently destructive.

The act of running counter to God's law is sometimes justified on the ground of "self-expression". It
certainly is not an expression of the self, for God, who
made the self, has declared that such action is contrary
to its nature. And a man who commits sin—any sin
—is to that extent less of a man, just as a motor car,
whose engine has been used in violation of its maker's
instructions, is less of a motor car. To return to the
argument of an earlier chapter—freedom results only
from doing what one ought. The connection between
law and freedom is absolute.

Yet we sin. Our will is so made that it can choose only
what appears to us as good. But two different and contradictory things may both appear to us as good from
different points of view: to abstain from meat on Friday is good because God's Church demands it; to eat

meat on Friday is good because our body is very fond of meat. Between these two goods the will can choose. Its tendency, since the fall, is to choose the more immediate, what we may call the nearer good—the one we like! To take a matter of more importance. If a married man falls in love with a woman who is not his wife, then two mutually exclusive courses of action will both seem to him, from different angles, good. To remain faithful to his own wife will seem good because God has forbidden adultery; to be faithless to her will seem good because his lower nature would find pleasure in the sin. Again the will must choose. And its tendency, against which it must struggle, is likely to be in the direction of the lower pleasure. Temptation—however tremendous—is not sin. It is not even venial sin. But for the will to yield to it, to choose the sin—even if it never proceeds to action—that is sin—as offence against God and a contradiction of one's own nature.

Vocation

What has been said so far in this chapter concerns law as an expression of God's general will for all men equally. But there is likewise a will of God for each individual, what is called his vocation. Shall a man be a priest or a layman? If a priest, shall he be a secular priest or a member of a religious community? These questions are momentous. Within the priesthood, there is almost every variety of way of serving God, opening for every type of character to proceed to its fullest development. If he is to be a layman, in which of the various ways of life open to him will he best serve God's purpose for him? To take one crucial question—shall he marry or not? Marriage, God teaches, is a high and holy state: normally men and women are called to it, for it is the race's duty to carry itself on. But though it is the race's duty, it is not the duty of every individual. Celibacy, chosen for God's sake (not mere celibacy, be it noted, but a celibacy definitely dedicated to God) is a higher and holier state still. It is part of the rule of life for priests. But, exceptionally, it may be God's will for a particular man or woman living in the world.

Now there is no organ in the Church for the expression of this vocation, no official to whom one may go for an official answer. It is the most intimate of matters between God and each soul. Nor is there any one way in which God guides all souls. In some cases, circumstances arise when the sense of vocation seems to point one way and circumstances another. In all such matters, there is possibility of self-deception, and the individual prays for clear guidance and takes the advice of experienced men.

In every case, of course, the individual vocation must be completely in accord with God's law for all men, and the existence of this general moral law is a strong aid to the clear perception of God's will for the individual.

LAW AND SUFFERING

THE RESISTANCE TO SIN nearly always involves some degree of suffering: in some cases it involves terrible suffering. And there are those who would relax the moral law when the suffering caused by obedience to it appears to be extreme.

Now, no one can alter God's law. Even the Church cannot do that: within the framework of his law, she may make what we call by-laws, binding upon her members, but these must be in accord with God's law, which she cannot change.

This point is not always grasped. The Church has received from God the power to make laws binding upon her members. But this power, as I have said, is subordinate to the laws stated by God himself as binding upon men. The distinction may be illustrated in the case of marriage. The Church cannot grant any of her children a divorce because when they make the contract of marriage (that is to say, agree to take each other as husband and wife for life) God brings into being a new relationship. Now, by God's act consequent upon their contract, they are man and wife. This new relationship, though it follows upon their contract, is not created by their contract, but by God. The Church can no more make them cease to be husband and wife than it could make a father and son cease to be father and son. But within the law laid down by God, the Church *can* legislate. It can, for instance, decree that for the marriage of a Catholic, the presence of a priest as witness is necessary. These laws being its own the Church can alter. But she cannot alter the laws given to her by God to be taught to men. Nor does she want to.

First, and most obviously, this is because of the nature of the law, as already set out. As it stands, God's law is a statement by man's maker of the right way for men to act. It is an expression of God's knowledge, and for human knowledge to try and change it would be absurd. Human institutions may try to alter the law out of pity for suffering men, but the law they are trying to alter is the law given by one who is Infinite Love.

But even if God's law were a lesser thing than that, the effort of men to make it easier would still be futile. No one but the law-maker can alter the law. If anyone else claims to, it is of no avail. For at the end of life, it is the law-maker who is to judge us, and he will judge us according to his laws as he made them, not according to the modifications introduced into his laws by men. It is as though one were doing an examination paper and some kindly soul, entering the room and discovering that we were in difficulties, altered the questions to make them easier for us. His act would undoubtedly make the writing of our paper easier, but it might make the reading of the examination results less pleasant.

But there is something worse than mere futility in this altering the moral law to reduce suffering. To make clear what it is we must look a little more closely into the nature of suffering.

Suffering is not necessarily an evil. As we have seen, a thing is evil if it hinders a being in the attainment of the purpose for which the being exists. In the fullest sense, therefore, a thing is evil for man only if it makes it more difficult for him to save his soul. Now suffering does not necessarily do so. Only sin is always and necessarily an evil.

Ordinary observation of life shows that suffering may work in two ways. First, it may be good for the sufferer: we know that a man who has never known suffering is soft and undeveloped. His character lacks substance. Immaturity clings about him. And not only do we find that this minimum of suffering is apparently necessary for man's proper development, we also find that really great suffering, if it has been dominated, has the power of enriching the character of the man or woman who has suffered. Suffering, if it ruins some characters, enriches others. It is not necessarily an evil, but may be an immense factor for good. Which it is to be depends, for every man, on the way he accepts it. It lies in him to dominate it or to be dominated by it.

Life is a period of testing: the suffering that arises
in it is part of that test. Suffering may be either curable or incurable. If it is physically incurable, a man
must put up with it: he has no choice. If it is curable,
but only by a breach of the moral law, a man need
not put up with it, he has a choice; yet he is morally
bound to put up with it. These two sorts of suffering
—the sort that cannot be avoided at all and the sort
that cannot be avoided without sin—represent the test
that God allows every man to go through. Every man
has not the same test: some men have more suffering
than others, but no man is allowed by God to have
more than he can, with the aid of God's grace, bear.
Part of the Christian law is love of neighbour, and the
relief of suffering is one of the noblest expressions of
this love. But it must be within the limits of God's
law.

Thus the effort of men to relax the moral law so
that others shall not suffer unduly is aimed at altering
the test devised by God himself. And there is another
thing. Life is not only a testing to see if a man is fit,
it is likewise a preparation to make him fit. Suffering,
as we have seen, can immensely enrich the soul. And
the whole of life represents God's means of bringing
a soul to its highest point of development. It is for
God to measure the amount of suffering necessary for
a man's perfection. And anyone who tries to modify
God's law in order to reduce the suffering is ensur-
ing that the soul shall not become as fine a thing as
it might. Steel is a beautiful thing, but it has taken an

immense heat to bring it to its right perfection. Anyone who, as it were in kindness, cut down the heat to half, would prevent the metal from ever being more than a useless mess. Some suffering is necessary: God knows how much each man needs; and it is by the suffering that cannot be legitimately avoided that God shows the measure of what is necessary.

The essence of the conquest of suffering is that it should be voluntary. Now the suffering that one could avoid by committing sin is obviously, in the strictest sense, voluntary. One has exercised a choice. But the suffering that one cannot avoid at all may equally be made voluntary: a man can accept it as coming from God's hands, thank God for it as the means by which God is choosing to fit his soul for its eternal destiny, and offer it to God for his own sins and the sins of other men.

When man has thus voluntarily accepted suffering, he has made one of the greatest of human conquests. For men naturally flee from suffering in fear of it. By an act of one's will to accept what all men flee from is in itself a triumph. But to go further—as the saints have done and many who are less than saints—and inflict suffering upon oneself—that is the supreme triumph over human weakness: for it is a positive going out to seek what other men flee from.

This infliction of suffering is not, of course, a mere aimless love of suffering. Nor does it arise, as some asceticisms have arisen, from hatred of the body or any feeling of the body's worthlessness. It has the immediate practical end of helping to bring the body into proper subordination to the soul—for a body not subordinate can ruin the whole being and fail to achieve its proper freedom as a body. But mortification has another significance that can be no more than touched on here. As there was a suffering of Christ's natural body, so there is a suffering of his Mystical Body. The human member can unite his suffering with Christ's and offer them for the whole body. "I fill up in my flesh", says Saint Paul, "what is wanting to the suffering of Christ for his body which is the church."

Human life, then, we may see as the preparing for the life of heaven. It means, on the one hand, complete self-conquest. The soul must conquer the body and bring it into full obedience to God's law; and the soul must itself come into full submission to God. It has, from God's Church, the truths it needs to know about God and man and its own destiny: from the same source it has the law that will govern it in the right use of itself and in the right relation of love and duty to others. But, as has been seen, given that man is to live a life above his nature, he needs those gifts above his nature which we call the Supernatural Life. In the next two chapters I shall discuss the Life.

THE SUPERNATURAL LIFE

How It Comes to the Soul

THE GROUND of the map is now sketched in. The end of the road of life is heaven, and death is a gateway on the road. God has given us means of knowing all that mass of truth by which we know what God and man are, what life and death mean, what conduct will bring man to heaven. Yet truth and law by themselves do not say all. Man's destiny is above his nature and therefore nothing in his nature will fit him for it. Something must be added to his nature to elevate it. Since what he has to do is to live the life of heaven—a life that his nature as such does not possess the power to live—he must receive the necessary powers from outside. And, as we have seen, he must receive them in this life. These powers, which enable the soul to live a life above its nature, flow from the possession of the Supernatural Life. In this chapter and the next, the Supernatural Life will be discussed. In this, the main question will be the way in which the soul receives it; in the next, the question will be what its effects are in the soul.

First, then, as to the way the soul receives it. In an earlier chapter, our Lord's phrase "I am the Life" was worked out fully. Here I shall repeat the main points very briefly. If Christ *is* the Life, then *he* must live in us; and that he really does so, Saint Paul bears witness when he says, "I live, yet now not I, but Christ liveth in me." The idea of one being living in another is already familiar to us in the case of the cells of the body; here the cells are living cells: yet they live not with some independent life of their own but with the life of the whole body. The cells of my body live with my life: it is I that live in them. This is shown to be more than a suggestive comparison by Saint Paul's clear working out of the idea of the Church as Christ's Body. The Church is a body, a living thing, as truly united to Christ as his natural body was upon this earth. He is the Head, the directing principle, union with which is a condition of life in the Body; and every member of the Church is a cell in the body and, as such, lives with the life of Christ, whose Body the Church is. This membership of Christ's Body—what we call incorporation with Christ —is the condition on which he can live in us. Only if we are members of a Church thus vitally united with him does his life flow through us.

We are incorporated—built into the Mystical Body —by baptism. We speak of baptism as a rebirth, a being born again. And rightly. Birth means entry into life. By birth we enter into the life of man. By rebirth we enter into the life of Christ; equally, the life of Christ enters into us. Thus our Lord himself says of baptism: "Unless a man be *born again* of water and the Holy Spirit, he shall not enter into the Kingdom of Heaven."

Prayer

Now the very first condition of human life, whether in the Body or out of it, is prayer. Prayer is simply the directing of life to God. Of prayer, thus understood, the most direct form is the turning of the soul to God that it may speak to him. This is not, as is sometimes thought, the whole of prayer, since every action of a life directed to God is a prayer. The proportion between this more direct form of prayer that consists in speaking to God and the less direct form that consists in work done for God's glory, is different for different men according to God's special will for each. At one end is the contemplative life, which is almost wholly direct prayer; at the other end is the active life, but this can and should be prayer also. In any case, if direct speaking to God is not the whole of prayer, it is prayer at its highest and must underlie all the rest. What have men to say to God? Endless things. But they may be grouped under four headings.

There is first *adoration*. It is of the nature of an intelligent being to honour excellence. God is supreme excellence, and man's intellect is therefore false to itself if it denies him its homage. Second, there is *thanksgiving*: we owe all things whatsoever to God and the failure to acknowledge it is literally fraudulent. Third, there is *sorrow for sin*. Fourth, there is *petition*—asking for things—spiritual and material, for ourselves and others. Mere petition, without the other three elements, is a poor shadow of prayer. With them it is an act of real enrichment to the soul, since it expresses not only a right relation of man to God, but a right relation of our wishes to God's will: man is sufficiently certain of God's love to ask for what he wants; sufficiently certain, also, to be assured that God will not grant him what he wants if it would be against his truest interests.

Prayer, thus understood in its fourfold subject matter, may also be considered with regard to its *mode*. It must primarily be in the soul: if it is not an act of the knowledge and love of man's soul, then it is of no value at all. But, thus rooted and grounded in the soul, it will make a twofold use of the body. *First*, the body affects the soul; *second*, the soul expresses itself through the body. As an example of the body affecting the soul, a crucifix seen by the eye may help to fix the soul in meditation upon Calvary. As an example of the soul expressing itself through the body, a man meditating upon Calvary and so coming to see the horror of his own sinfulness in the light of the love of God, may find relief to the power of his soul's sorrow by falling on his knees or striking his breast. In a full life of prayer, then, the body will not be excluded. But there is a *third* thing. Man is not an isolated unit, but a being linked by his very nature to other men. He owes his coming into existence to a man and a woman; he owes his continuance in existence, the development of his powers of mind and body, the full life of his emotions, to a certain cooperation with others. If prayer is to be a directing of his life to God, this necessary social element in his nature must not be excluded—otherwise there would be a whole side of his nature not consecrated to God. Therefore not only must he pray for his fellow men, he must from time to time join with them in the worship of God. The man who never goes to church is not merely dispensing with a particular piece of ceremonial. He is refusing to join his fellows in God's worship.

This rough analysis of prayer—into the four kinds of things to be said to God and the three ways of saying them—does, as has already been noted, apply to all men, whether in the Church or out of it, whether aware or unaware of any revelation of God to man. It is an analysis based upon the very nature of God and man and is therefore of universal application. But it has special application to the Catholic. For his knowledge of God in Christ our Lord gives him all the more reason for adoration and thanksgiving and sorrow, all the more confidence in petition; and in every part of his prayer, a true ground of intimacy and personal contact. The use of the soul in prayer is the same for him as for all men; the use of the body is greater since he knows that God took to himself not only a human soul but a human body too; and the social element in prayer is inevitably stronger with men who realize that they are not only in a loose sense members of the human race, but in a strict sense cells of one living body and

so joined, not only to Christ but to all others, living
and dead, who are likewise cells of the Mystical Body
of Christ.

There is not only a prayer of the individual cell but
a prayer of the whole body. And if for its own individual prayer, the cell uses the life of the whole body,
equally it joins in the prayer of the whole body and
so makes it its own.

The Mass

What, then, is this prayer of the whole body? Obviously, it must be the prayer of the Head, of him whose
Body it is: that is, it must be the prayer of Christ. Here
again we come to something of quite vital importance
for the understanding of the Catholic scheme of life.
There is a powerful phrase in the Epistle to the He-
brews that may serve as a starting point for thought,
"Christ ever liveth to make intercession for us." This
involves several things: (1) Christ is in heaven, at the
right hand of the Father. (2) His intercession for us is
not a thing done upon Calvary once and for all, but
a continuous thing, a thing that never ceases. In other
words, Christ in heaven is unceasingly making intercession for us. (3) But the basis of our Lord's intercession is Calvary. That is what he is offering to his
Father on our behalf. Therefore, Christ in heaven is
continuously offering his own death upon Calvary to
his Father on our behalf. That is the prayer of Christ
himself.

The prayer of his Body is an earthly participation in that. The smallest individual prayer of every member of the Body is joined with, flows into, our Lord's continuous offering of Calvary: that, indeed, is the meaning of the phrase "through Jesus Christ our Lord", which is affixed in so many words to some of our prayers and belongs in idea to all of them. As with the individual prayer of the members, so with the prayer of the whole Body: it is a joining up with the continuous offering of Christ.

That being so, it is not surprising that it should find its highest point in the Mass, which is the exact projection here upon earth of the continuous offering in heaven. This truth is worth stating with some precision. In heaven, as we have seen, our Lord unceasingly offers himself, the Victim slain upon Calvary, for all men. In the Mass, our Lord offers himself, the Victim slain upon Calvary, for all men.

First, it is our Lord that makes the offering. He is acting through his Mystical Body as though through his natural body: it is therefore *his* offering, the Body simply being the instrument he uses. Thus every member of the Church is joined in the offering, but certain special members, the priests, have been given by God special powers enabling them to act for the Body. They are, in a sense, the immediate instrument. Thus three truths must be kept in mind: (1) Christ is the chief priest, offering himself by his own power; (2) the priest offers for the people by power granted him by Christ; (3) the people offer Christ's sacrifice through the priest.

Second, it is himself that our Lord is offering at Mass. On the night before his death, our Lord, at supper with his apostles, took bread and consecrated it so that, while retaining the appearance of bread, it ceased to be bread and became his Body, his real body, the body in which he walked the earth and was nailed upon the Cross. Likewise, he took wine and consecrated it so that, while retaining the appearance of wine, it ceased to be wine, and became his Blood. He gave his Body to the apostles to eat and his Blood to drink. And all that he had done, he empowered them to do. The apostles passed on the power, and to this day, in the Mass, the priests of the Church consecrate bread and wine so that they become the Body and Blood of Christ. And because the Body is the Body of the *living* Christ, where the body is, there is the living Christ in his totality—Man and God. And equally, where the Blood is, there is the living Christ in his totality. At Mass, the priest (acting as an instrument in the hands of Christ) offers Christ thus totally present. In other words, at the altar, Christ is offering himself, the Victim slain upon Calvary, but now ever living, just as in heaven he continuously offers himself, the Victim slain upon Calvary, but now ever living. The Mass is really heaven as it were breaking through to earth to be seen of men.

But the priest does not only consecrate, he also consumes: he receives our Lord, whole and living, into his body just as the apostles did. And the congregation likewise may receive him. This is Communion, the

Blessed Eucharist, receiving Christ himself into ourselves. "He that eateth me, the same shall live by me." The members of Christ's Mystical Body have as their proper food nothing less than Christ himself—"the Life". Other food gives life: this food *is* Life.

Our situation as Catholics may be seen in its simplest elements. By baptism, we are built into the Body of Christ, and as cells in the Body we are able to live with the life of the Body. The condition of all life in God is prayer: our prayer in the Body culminates in the supreme prayer of the Mass, and from the Mass we receive Christ himself to be the food of our life in the Body. Communion, then, is God's supreme gift to us upon earth. Everything in our life is vitalized by it. Baptism leads up to it, everything else flows from it.

The Sacraments

But there are other ways in which the life of Christ flows to the individual cell. Besides baptism and the Blessed Eucharist, our Lord instituted five other sacraments.

First a word as to sacraments. These are material things that are by God's power made to convey grace— or life—to the soul. We say of them that they are symbols, differing from other symbols in that they actually effect what they symbolize. Thus baptism—with its pouring of water on the body—is a symbol of cleansing, and it does cleanse the soul. The other five sacraments are confirmation, penance, holy orders, matrimony, and extreme unction [now known as anointing of the sick].

A very brief word of these individually: confirmation and holy orders are linked with baptism in that they can only be received once, because, as it is phrased, they confer a character on the soul, which means that they confer some share in the priesthood of our Lord. Baptism makes a man a member of Christ; confirmation gives him the right and the duty to defend the Mystical Body of Christ; holy orders makes him a priest, confers upon him among other things the power to offer the sacrifice of the Mass and to absolve from sin. The fullness of the priesthood is in the bishop, who has certain further powers, including those of confirming and ordaining. But whether priest or bishop, the point to be held firmly is that the man is not acting of himself, but of his own will gives himself to be used as an instrument by Christ. What is done through him, Christ does and no other; so that his moral character, whatever effect it may have on his own salvation, has no effect at all on the sacramental work Christ uses him to do. To hold otherwise would actually be to place a man between us and God. If his moral character could affect the grace we receive, then it would be in some way derived from the priest and not wholly from God.[1]

---

[1] There are two truths that must be seen in proper relation: (1) the priest is simply an instrument in the hands of Christ; yet (2) as minister of the sacrament, he must have the right intention. According to

Of the others, *penance* is the sacrament of the forgiveness of sins. A man receives the Supernatural Life
at baptism, he can lose it only by a deliberate act of rebellion against God—what is called a mortal sin: mortal because it brings death, for death is the loss of life
and by mortal sin the soul loses the Supernatural Life.
The Life thus lost is regained when we receive the
sacrament of penance, when, that is, with true sorrow
for having offended God, we confess our sins to his
priest, and from the priest as God's instrument, receive

---

the first, the sacrament does not flow from the priest but from Christ
and the sacrament is not affected in the faintest way by the priest's
character—neither gaining from his holiness nor suffering loss from
his sins. According to the second, the priest, simply withholding his
intention, can prevent the sacrament from taking place. The priest's
character cannot affect the sacrament, yet his intention can. At first
sight this may seem a contradiction. But it is not so. The priest is
an instrument: that is, he gives certain of his human acts, and these
are used by God as channels of grace. But for a complete human act,
intention is necessary. The act a man does not intend cannot be called
his act at all. Therefore if a priest has the true intention, God uses him
—*as an instrument*, God doing the work. But if the priest withholds
his intention, God cannot use him as a sacramental instrument and
nothing happens at all.

The question "How can a bad priest administer a sacrament?"
misses the point. In this sense, there is no such thing as a bad priest.
There are priests who are bad men, just as there are doctors who are
bad men. But as one only calls a man a bad doctor if he practises
medicine badly, so one can only call a man a bad priest if he does his
work badly. But, in the case in point, priestly work consists simply
in giving certain of his acts that can be used by God sacramentally.
Provided he does this, he does all that the holiest man can do. If he
does not do this, there is no sacrament at all.

God's forgiveness and the return of the Supernatural Life to the soul.

Matrimony is the sacrament of the entry upon the married state. When two people marry, they take each other as husband and wife for life—this, whether they are baptized or not. If they are baptized, then their marriage is a sacrament—a means whereby God's grace flows to their souls to give them the aids they need for the sanctification of their life together and the overcoming of such difficulties as may arise in it. It is to be noted that the priest does not administer this sacrament to the parties, they administer it to each other.

Extreme unction, the Last Anointing [anointing of the sick], is the sacrament for grievous illness and the danger of death.

But all these other sacraments draw their efficacy from their relation to the central sacrament, the Blessed Eucharist. And this is not a mere chance. Prayer and the sacraments are both means of life. In prayer, man approaches God. In the sacraments, God approaches man. But both culminate in the same point. For the highest prayer is the Mass, and the highest sacrament is the Eucharist. Thus at the point where man's approach to God reaches its uttermost intensity, God's response is at its most measureless richness.

It is to be noted in the sacramental system how closely God has followed the lines of human life. *First*, observe that the very nature of the sacrament is a representation of the nature of man: man is the union of a body and soul, that is, of matter and spirit. God chooses to act upon him by means that are likewise a union of matter and spirit.

Second, observe that the sacraments bear the same relation to life as a glove to the hand—they are made to fit it. The natural life of man has certain fixed points: he is born, grows to manhood, marries or becomes a priest, dies. Roughly corresponding to these five points are five sacraments: baptism, confirmation, matrimony or holy orders, extreme unction. Beyond these five points there are two things to be considered: man sins, and for that there is the sacrament of penance, and running through all is daily life—and for that there is the appropriate food, the Blessed Eucharist. Thus provision is made for man's sanctification not only in his individual life, but also in his relation to the community—on its social side by matrimony, on its religious side by holy orders.

Third, observe that the sacraments are built upon the natural life in still another way: they make use of four everyday things—bread, water, wine, oil—and two everyday situations—the exercise of authority and marriage. Now to these four common things and two common situations, the natural life might be reduced in its simplest elements.

Throughout, then, the sacramental system is a reminder of two things: (1) that matter and spirit are not eternally at enmity, but that matter may be the vehicle of spirit—a truth taught at its very highest in the fact of the Incarnation itself, when God took to himself a human body and made it his own;[2] (2) that the Supernatural Life does not abolish the natural life and take its place, but enters into the natural life and supernaturalizes it.

Here then is man: a member of Christ's Mystical Body by baptism, open to the inpouring of the Supernatural Life.

The Indwelling of the Holy Spirit

But there is another great truth about man's membership of the Mystical Body. Our Lord, while constantly speaking of himself as the Life, also speaks of the Holy Spirit whom he is to send and associates him most intimately with the continuing work of man's salvation. Saint Paul speaks almost interchangeably of life in Christ and life in the Holy Spirit. When Christ promised to live in us, something more was involved than our sharing the life of his human nature. For he was God. And, therefore, since we are united organically with Christ as Head, we are indwelt by the Blessed Trinity. But we have already seen, the princi-

[2] This consecration of matter, seen in the Incarnation and in the Church's sacraments, is carried to its furthest conclusion in the Church's practice with regard to what is called sacramentals. These, unlike the sacraments, are not instituted by our Lord, but by the Church. Yet they follow from our Lord's own practice. As he blessed bread before he ate it, so the Church blesses the material things man uses in his daily life and further attaches her blessing to material things (as in holy water) and material actions (as in the sign of the Cross) man may use in his prayer. In all these cases, material things are brought into the full stream of the Church's prayer and so into a special relationship with God.

ple of appropriation by which the works of sanctification are especially associated with the Holy Spirit. It is by the power of the Holy Spirit that God became man in his Mother's womb; and it is by the power of the Holy Spirit that man is reborn into the Mystical Body —"unless a man be born again of water and the Holy Spirit, he cannot enter into the Kingdom of heaven." When he was giving his apostles the power to forgive sins, he breathed upon them and said: "Receive ye the Holy Spirit": the Holy Spirit came upon the apostles in the upper room and sent them forth for the conversion of the world: by Christ's own word, the Holy Spirit, the Comforter, was to abide with his Church. Everything the Church does for the sanctification of her individual member, every step that a member takes in supernatural development, is attributed to the third Person of the Blessed Trinity.

12

THE SUPERNATURAL LIFE

How It Works in the Soul

I N THE LAST CHAPTER, the channels by which the Supernatural Life come to the soul were dealt with.
In this we must consider the Life itself and its effects
upon the soul. It is to be observed how careful Scripture is to make clear that grace—the gift of the Supernatural Life—does not destroy nature, but elevates
it. "I make all things new", says Christ, not "I make
all new things." What he said of the law of Moses—
"I come not to destroy but to fulfill"—he might have
said of human nature. He took human nature and into
it poured a new thing, thus renewing it, making it new.
He did not give new faculties to the soul, but he gave
the existing faculties of intellect and will new powers
of action, powers to act above their natural level. Here
again we must follow very closely if we are to grasp
the real nature of our road.

Man by nature is a union of body and soul. The
soul has two faculties—the intellect and the will. Now
every faculty of man has first its own proper *action*;

and second its own proper *object*. Thus the eye has its action—namely, to see—and its object—namely, coloured surface. So the intellect has its action, which is *to know* or be aware of, and its object, which is *truth*. Likewise, the will has its action, which is *to love*, and its object, which is *goodness*. In other words, the intellect knows things insofar as they appear to the soul true, and the will loves things insofar as they appear to the soul good. Now the supreme truth is God, so the intellect's highest task is to know God. And the supreme goodness is God, so the will's highest task is to love God. The natural life of man's soul might be set out as follows:

	FACULTY	ACTION	OBJECT	SUPREME OBJECT
Soul {	Intellect	. . to know	. . truth	. . God
	Will	. . to love	. . goodness	. . God

Thus if we had no revelation from God as to his purpose in creating man, we might deduce from the study of man's nature that he was meant to know and to love God. And this answer would be, as a mere matter of words, correct. But it would be wrong in fact: for it would not rise above the knowing and loving proper to our nature, and God has revealed to us that our destiny is to know him directly, face to face, and to love him according to that knowledge. For this, as we have seen, we need new powers, and God gives us these by grace.

When grace comes in, intellect and will are supernaturalized—that is, their nature is not destroyed but given the power of higher action. The *intellect* retains its object, namely, truth, but its action is elevated; in other words, it can get at truth in a higher way: it can now believe upon the word of God, that is, it has the supernatural virtue of *faith*. The will likewise retains its object—namely, goodness—but its action is elevated from love in the natural order to supernatural love; that is, it has the supernatural virtue of *charity*, by which it loves God and makes the love of God the root of all its other loves and therefore of all its other actions. And the will is rendered capable of another supernatural action—the action of *hope*: that is, of aspiring to God in reliance upon his power and his goodness. The Supernatural Life of man's soul might then be set out as follows:

FACULTY	VIRTUE	ACTION	OBJECT [1]
Soul { Intellect . .	faith	. . to believe	. . . God
Will . . . . { hope	. . to hope	. . . God
charity	. . to love	. . . God

Yet the full activity of the Supernatural Life is not in this world. Its completion is in the next. The *intellect* will then see God directly: it will know him face to face. This direct seeing of God is by a double title supernatural. No created being—man or angel—could

[1] It will be noted that God is not here shown as the *supreme* object of faith, hope and charity, but as their object. He is their sole object; they have no other. Hence their name—the theological virtues.

by his own powers have direct vision of God, the gulf between Creator and creature being measureless. And man cannot by his own powers have direct vision of anything at all. For man knows things by means of ideas: when I claim to know another person, I mean that a certain idea and image of him is present in my mind and not the man himself. It is by means of this idea and image that I know him. But in heaven, we shall know God directly, not by means of an idea in the mind. So that faith will disappear and direct knowledge will take its place. For the intellect of man there are three levels of action, all having truth as their object: first, natural knowledge; second (for the man in a state of grace here below), faith; third (for the soul in heaven), direct knowledge. To this we shall return in the final chapter of this book. Here simply note that in heaven faith will be no more, for vision will be unclouded; hope will have yielded to possession; only charity will remain—the love binding man to God. But, since love and knowledge are closely connected, charity in heaven will have a newness of intensity proportioned to the new direct knowledge.

To return to this world: the soul in a state of grace —that is, possessed of the Supernatural Life—has the three virtues of faith, hope, and charity. But, as has already been said, it can lose the Supernatural Life. It does so by mortal sin—that is, by a deliberate and willful rejection of God. It has to be remembered that man's nature is a damaged nature. The sin of Adam did not render human nature totally evil. But it *did* leave it with a tendency or bias toward evil—a tendency to seek its own interest rather than God's will and a tendency to judge of its own interest by the vivid picturing of the imagination and not by the judgment of the reason. Grace does not of itself remove this unhappy bias. Man's nature is by grace given powers to act above its own level; yet it retains that uneasy pull toward self-interest and the too-dominant imagination. Grace helps it, principally, because these three new modes of action bring God closer and clearer. But the bias in the nature is cured only by steady striving to work with grace toward the will of God. And the striving may be marred by many a yielding—the lesser yielding of venial sin, the graver yielding of deliberate rejection of God for self. By such an act, the bond of love is broken (for one cannot at the same time love God and be in rebellion against him): in technical language, the soul loses the virtue of charity. The soul in mortal sin thus *necessarily* loses charity: it may retain hope and faith,[2] but without charity, hope and faith are not supernaturally alive and cannot sanctify the soul. The Supernatural Life and the virtue of charity are inseparable: the one cannot be without the other.

Thus the *first* result of the possession of the Super-

[2] Faith, hope, and charity being habits are only destroyed by actions contrary to them. Mortal sin—being rejection of God—is contrary to love of God and therefore means the loss of charity. But it is not necessarily contrary to faith and hope. Hope will be lost as a result of a mortal sin directly contrary to it—e.g., despair—and faith likewise by a mortal sin directly contrary to it—e.g., unbelief.

natural Life is that in this life we have access to God by these three paths—faith, hope, charity—all of them totally above the *natural* powers of our soul.

A *second* result is that man is enabled to perform actions that will merit a supernatural reward. The life of heaven, be it remembered, is a life above our nature. Therefore we could never merit it by our own natural powers. Natural action could obviously never merit a supernatural reward. Only if we are supernaturalized and thus made capable of acting above our nature can we merit a reward above our nature. For a soul in a state of grace, this is simple enough. What of a soul that lacks the Supernatural Life, either having lost it or never having had it? Such a soul has only the natural life and as such can make no step supernaturally. If it is to be enabled so to act as to gain —or regain—the Supernatural Life, it must receive a special "impulse" from God. Such an "impulse" is called actual grace. This must be distinguished from the sanctifying grace—or Supernatural Life—we have been treating of so far. Sanctifying grace is really a quality given to the soul, elevating it from within, abiding with the soul till it is lost by sin. Actual grace does not abide with the soul, does not sanctify it. It is God moving the soul, giving it a kind of impetus, enabling it to perform some supernatural act —of faith, or trust, or fear—that by its own nature it could not perform. If the soul responds to actual grace and makes the appropriate supernatural act, it receives sanctifying grace. To put it in another way, if the soul responds to supernatural impulse it receives Supernatural Life.

A *third* result is, as has already been stated many times, that man's soul is *fitted* for the life of heaven.

A *fourth* result is that men by grace become sons of God. By birth we are creatures of God, servants of God, but not sons. Once we receive the Supernatural Life, we have received that which will one day enable us to know him directly. But it is proper to God's own nature—and to no other—to know God directly. Thus, by a gift of God, we are enabled to do something that belongs to God's own nature, hence there is a real similitude of nature rightly expressed by the word "sons". This is what Saint Peter means when he says that we shall be made partakers of the divine nature; and the Church expresses the same truth when she says that grace is a "created participation in the life of God".

Any man possessed of the Supernatural Life is of necessity possessed also of faith, hope, and charity. There is no limit to the degree of intensity of the life. By baptism we receive it. If by mortal sin we lose it, then by the sacrament of penance we regain it. By the Blessed Eucharist principally, it receives addition. By prayer and by meritorious action of every kind man obtains from God increase of the Supernatural Life. And the whole purpose of man's life upon earth might be stated as the obtaining, preserving, and increasing of this life of grace in his soul.

We are now at last in a position to take stock of the

life of the member of Christ's Church. The primary
fact about him is that he is not an isolated unit, pur-
suing his own solitary path to his own private goal.
He is a cell in a living Body, the Body of Christ. As
such he has a special relation to Christ: for Christ's life
flows through every cell in his Mystical Body. The cell
—that is to say, the individual Catholic—may yield
his will wholly to Christ, or partially, or not at all;
and, according to which of these he chooses to do,
he will have the Life flowing through him in pleni-
tude, or less fully or not at all. For a man can be a
dead cell in the Body, retaining faith, but not vivified by charity, for the Supernatural Life is inseparable
from the virtue of charity, which is love. But insofar
as his will is right, then Christ lives in him; and because Christ, then the Holy Spirit likewise: the Spirit
of God, proceeding from the Father and the Son, in
his own adorable essence the bond of love between
Father and Son and so ever known by the Church as
the Giver of Life. Thus the member of the Church,
living supernaturally, is indwelt by the Holy Spirit, organically united to Christ who is God the Son, and
by him brought to the Father.

The relation of all the redeemed to Christ involves a
relation of all to each other. The one life flows through
them all: all are sharing in the divine life that pours
out from the Head. So that whether in heaven or in
Purgatory or upon earth, all members of Christ are
members of one another. And as in a body, one part
can help another because of the life it has, so in the

Church, one person can help another because of the life that flows to him from the Head. Thus when our Lady obtains graces for us by her prayers, she is acting not by her own power, but by virtue of the life that is in her from Christ—a life that is also in us, though in her the life is a thousandfold more intense because of the greater perfection of her love of God here upon earth.

This life in the Body is the first thing to be noted. Every member of the Body who is not in rebellion against God possesses it, as it were, automatically. Normally, also, though not automatically, he possesses two other things, only less important than the Life: for, as a member of the Church, he has the means of knowing the laws God has made for right conduct and all the truths that will enable him to understand the meaning and purpose of his life. Thus he knows all that mass of truth concerning God (who made him and who rules him and to whom he must come) that have already been indicated and principally he knows that God is love—a piece of knowledge that is a most powerful stimulus to right action of every kind and that, as has been seen, marks the supreme difference between Christianity and all other religions whatsoever. He knows, further, all sorts of truths about himself: including the damage wrought in his nature by the sin of the first man, which makes of every man, be he never so great a saint, a kind of convalescent—one, that is, on the road to health but weakened in constitution and not secure from relapse until he enters heaven. He knows how the original weakness of his nature (which he cannot help) and the damage caused by his own sins (which he *can* help) may be repaired. He knows the meaning of sin—both in its attraction for himself and in its ugliness before God. He knows something of the meaning of suffering and knows, therefore, how it may be used for the eternal enrichment of his own soul and offered to God for the souls of others. He knows that in a world ruled over by the providence of God nothing is of necessity evil, save only sin.

In the mere detail of his life, he has the supreme advantage of possessing a standard by which all things can be judged. His own career in life, his love of his neighbour, his duties to his neighbour, the entangled claims upon him of family, nation, humanity at large: in judging of all these, he can apply principles, where other men can only be puzzled by a crowd of instincts or emotions. For in a tremendous number of instances, the law of God is quite explicit, so that no discussion arises; and where he cannot clearly hear the law of God, he knows what man is made for and can at any rate make the effort to judge by that: Is this or that condition of things helpful to the saving of men's souls, or a hindrance? Once this primary matter is settled, other considerations—as to his own and his neighbour's temporal well-being—must receive attention. But urgent as such questions may be, they can never be his first concern.

For every man, the one really vital thing is that he should have the Supernatural Life in his soul, for one day he will die.

13

HELL

M AN, WE SAY, is a union of spirit and matter. The soul animates the body. But there comes a time when the body is no longer capable of responding to the soul's animating power. The soul is as powerful as ever, but the body has deteriorated—whether by the sudden destruction of some essential part or by the gradual wearing down of age. When that moment comes, the body ceases to be vivified by the soul and falls away into corruption. The soul, being a spirit, does not cease. It ceases to animate the body, but its other powers—of knowledge and will—are still in action. The soul lives on, awaiting the moment when, by God's act, the body is to be reunited to it and man thereby reconstituted in his complete humanity for all eternity.

Death is not at the end of life. Yet there is a finality about death. It closes the first period of man's life, and this period, though not in itself permanent, is decisive of all that is to come. It is not the end of life. But it is the end of the road. After it man has arrived, and

there is no further journeying for him. This life upon
earth is a period of preparation. At the end of it, man
has *become* something: the something he has become
he will eternally remain.

The decisive factor is his will. From the beginning
of man's life upon earth, God is the supreme object of
the love of man's will when this is rightly directed. Yet
during life upon earth, there is in most men a good deal
of fluctuation, and in all men at least the possibility of
fluctuating. At one moment the will is set toward God.
Then comes mortal sin and the will is set toward self
and away from God. With repentance and true sorrow,
the will is turned again to God. And so it goes on.
But with death the fluctuations of the will are over: it
has chosen finally and will not change. This power of
the will to make a final choice it will not change—
a power that makes possible not only the eternity of
hell but also the eternity of heaven—anyone might at
least suspect from reflection upon the experiences of
this life. Character tends to set into a mould, the way
of life to become settled as the years go by. We might,
as I say, suspect that at death the will has made final
choice of its direction. From God's teaching we know
that it *has* done so. It is either fixed toward God or
fixed away from God: that is to say, man either loves
God with a love that will abide forever or hates God
with a hatred equally abiding. In the one case, he will
spend eternity with God. In the other case, he will
spend eternity apart from God.

It is easy to see how all this applies to the Catholic. By baptism he is incorporated with Christ—that is to say, he becomes a living cell in Christ's Mystical Body. As such he is living with the Supernatural Life of Christ, just as in every man the cells of his body live with his life. But membership of Christ does not automatically mean living with the life of Christ. While the will of the individual remains united with the will of God, the life of Christ pours into his soul, and he remains supernaturally alive. But if the individual sets his will against God, he cuts off the flow of the life of Christ. He remains (during his life upon earth) a member of the Body: but he is not sharing in the life of the Body. He lives with his natural life as a man, but supernaturally he is not alive.

The ending of our life upon earth will then find us either with the Supernatural Life, with our wills united to God, or without the Supernatural Life, with our wills set away from God. The one state means heaven, the other hell.

It is necessary to be very clear about hell. I have said that if a man dies hating God, then he must be separated from God. But it may be urged that hatred of God is rare. Explicit hatred of God may be rare, but there is a form of self-love that is equivalent to it. Thus a man might go through life ignoring God— and therefore not hating him—but building up such a love of self that he has only to be confronted with God to hate him. After death, God cannot be ignored; and then love of self will bring to the surface that hate of God which has always been implicit in it and of which the only possible consequence is separation from God.

This separation is everlasting. Enough has already been said to show why: it is everlasting because the state of will that produces it is everlasting. A man goes on through all eternity hating God. Therefore, through all eternity he remains separated from God. There is only one barrier between himself and God—his own hatred of God; but that barrier he will not tear down. Thus since his will is fixed in hatred of God, there is nothing to be done. Obviously he cannot be united to God, whom he hates: he must therefore remain separated.

Here, then, is a man with his will fixed irrevocably against God. What follows? In the first place, he has sinned and has not repented: justice demands then that he be punished. In hell he receives punishment from God: that there is punishment, and that it is great, we know, but how great and whether or not it is unrelaxing, we do not know.

But there is a second, more terrible consideration. He is, as we have seen, eternally separated from God. But he needs God, his nature was made for God. Whenever we are deprived of something that our nature needs, we suffer. From that rule there is no escape. If we are deprived of food, we suffer the agonies of hunger. If we are deprived of drink, we suffer the far worse agonies of thirst. But our whole nature needs God far more than our bodies need food and drink. If, then, a man is deprived of God, he must, inescapably, suffer, and this with the greatest suffering possible to man. And whereas death comes to end the agonies of hunger and thirst, the man in hell cannot die. He is deprived for all eternity of what his nature needs, *and deprived by the inflexible choice of his own will.* If any soul in hell would turn to God and ask for mercy, God would grant his prayer. But the souls in hell will not ask. They hate their suffering, but they hate God more. With their love of evil and their hatred of God, heaven would be a fiercer torment than hell. It is the tragedy of final impenitence that it puts the sinner beyond the reach of help. There is nothing that *can* be done for him. He has perverted his own nature and there is therefore no possible condition of happiness for him. Hell is bad. Heaven would be worse. What keeps him in hell is not the insatiable vengeance of God, but the unchanging direction of his own will toward evil. The will of man is free to make its choice: God does not interfere with that freedom. Those who have hoped that the souls in hell might one day be saved have assumed that those souls would one day turn from evil to good. We know, because God has told us, that they will never do so. They have *become* something—their will has fixed itself, for ever, in the hatred of God. Given the purpose of man's life, these men have failed.

It is worth noting that our Lord is very insistent upon the reality of hell. In the best-known passage of all he describes himself as saying to sinners at the Last Day: "Depart from Me, ye cursed, into the everlasting fire that was prepared for the devil and his angels." In this passage are contained the three truths about hell that have already been set down: that it involves separation from God ("Depart from Me"); that it involves punishment ("fire"); that it is *everlasting* fire. And there is the further assertion that the souls of the damned in hell will be in the company of those angels who, like them, fixed their wills in eternal enmity with God.

Apart from this passage, however, our Lord is constantly referring to it. In the Sermon on the Mount, for instance, he reminds sinners of hell six separate times. And this fact is worth weighing by those who would dismiss the doctrine as contradicting the divine love. For no one would question Christ's love for men: yet the doctrine is undoubtedly his. There is, it is true, a mystery in the fact of hell: but it is not a mystery of God's cruelty; it is a mystery of the human will with its possibility of fixing itself in evil.

14

PURGATORY: HEAVEN

T HOSE WHO THUS DIE with their wills fixed *against* God find their eternal abiding place instantly. What of those whose wills are united to him? It will be remembered that here a distinction must be made. The life of Christ does not vivify every living cell in his Body with equal intensity. A living member of the Mystical Body may have his will either totally united or partially united with God's will. In the first case, he is totally living with the life of Christ, totally possessed by him, and at death passes instantly into heaven. In the second, there still remains something of self unsubjected to God. He loves God and his soul is indwelt by his Spirit. Yet imperfections remain. God holds the centre of the soul, but there are, as it were, outlying regions still not completely subject to him. Upon such a man sin still has a certain hold, and this usually in one of two ways: either there is venial sin not repented of or there is mortal sin, repented of yet not sufficiently.

Venial sin, of course, does not destroy the Supernatural Life of the soul, and therefore does not send a soul to hell: yet it remains a breach of God's law. As such, justice demands that it shall be punished like any other breach of God's law. Repentance of course would wipe out the debt of punishment. But venial sin is often slight enough, does not stir the soul, is forgotten almost at once; so that frequently there is no repentance, and at death the debt of justice stands.

The second condition is more delicate. When a man commits a mortal sin, he loses the Supernatural Life; when he is truly contrite he regains it. Now contrition is to be measured in two different ways: as to its motive and as to the degree of its intensity. If a man is *truly* contrite (that is, sorry, for the right motive) and *sufficiently* contrite (that is, as sorry as the gravity of the sin demands) then all is forgiven, guilt and punishment alike. But what of a man whose sorrow, while true and sincere, falls short of the necessary degree of intensity? The guilt of his sin *is* forgiven: the Supernatural Life is restored to his soul, and God allows him to make up by suffering for what is lacking in his sorrow: in other words, some punishment still remains, even after the guilt is forgiven.

If a man die in either of these states—with venial sin not repented of or mortal sin repented of but not sufficiently—there is still the debt of justice to be satisfied and the soul brought altogether to freedom from sin and union with God: and in Purgatory, by God's mercy, this cleansing and compensating suffering is undergone. The souls in Purgatory suffer, but the strife is over. They know that heaven is theirs.

It now only remains to consider the state of those who enter heaven, whether they enter it immediately upon death or after a space in Purgatory.

Heaven

Of heaven there is no need to speak at great length here, because heaven is the end of the road and was therefore treated in some fullness at the beginning of the map—in the third chapter. Scripture tells us three things very clearly: (1) The happiness of heaven is perfect—broken by no present sorrow and no fear of future ceasing. It is happiness of the whole being, the soul's every power acting at its very highest. (2) The happiness of heaven is indescribable and unimaginable. "Eye hath not seen, nor hath ear heard, nor hath it entered into the heart of man what things God hath prepared for them that love him." The language made by man from his experiences of this life has no power to convey the experiences of the next. The pictures of joy built by our imagination, fed upon the joys of this life, are poor shadows of the joy of heaven.

(3) But if by imagination we can take no grip on heaven's happiness, by the higher faculty of intellect —acting upon the revelation of God—we can know something of it. In heaven we shall see God "face to face"; we shall "know as we are known", so says Scripture. Which means that we shall know God, not, as we know things here below, by an idea in the mind, but directly, God himself present in our very soul and

realized by us as present, realized at the very highest point of intensity. This is what theology calls the Beatific Vision. "We shall be made like to Him," said Saint John, "for we shall see Him as He is."

Our soul, then, will have laid hold on God. God is supreme truth, so our intellect, with no barrier between itself and its supreme object, will be eternally enriched in eternal activity, for God is infinite and our intellect will never exhaust the truth that is its supreme beatitude. But God is also supreme goodness, so our will equally will find no barrier between itself and its supreme object and will come to rest in eternal love. Not all souls will be equal in heaven. The soul grows naturally by development of intellect and will. Supernaturally—which is what matters here—it grows by the possession of the Supernatural Life. But this it must receive upon earth, for after death it cannot merit. Therefore, souls united with God have not all reached the same degree of development when they come to die. But, greater or smaller, all souls are functioning in heaven with intellect and will at their highest intensity upon their highest object: therefore every soul will know perfect happiness. To summarize what has been said earlier: those very sundry qualities in the things of earth that cause us happiness are all caused by God, the Creator of all things; they are therefore already present in him, not in the shadowy and imperfect way in which we find them in created things, but complete and perfect in their highest form. Finding him, then, we find at an infinitely higher level all things whatsoever that have caused us happiness upon earth.

So much for the essentials of heaven—the direct apprehension of the Blessed Trinity. Bound up with that is a fellowship with all the other citizens of heaven: fellowship with Christ our Lord—the second Person of the Trinity made man—with his Mother, with the angels and saints. So that heaven is not only our relationship with God come to maturity, but also our relationship with all the lovers of God—with all created beings, that is, who have achieved the purpose for which God made them.

Here then, in the very briefest space, we have seen something of the world into which death ushers us. Yet if death ushers us into the next life, it does not choose our place: that is decided by the state of our soul in relation to God. That is what we call the "particular judgment"—the decision made at each man's death of the place to which each belongs. Till the world ends, we shall live in heaven simply as souls, separated from the bodies that once were ours. In heaven, Christ our Lord is bodily present, that the whole of human nature (not soul only, but the union of soul and body) in its perfection should be present at the right hand of the Father. His body is his natural body, yet glorified: without suffering, or deformity, no longer a cloak to the soul, but as it were translucent, so that the soul is only the brighter for the body it indwells. And similarly our Lady is bodily present too—so says the doctrine of the Assumption. But in the normal course of

God's providence, the souls in heaven must wait for the Last Day to be reunited to their bodies.

For there is a Last Day. As there is an end to every man's term upon earth, so there will one day be an end to the term upon earth of the human race. When the Mystical Body of Christ shall have grown to its full stature—"unto a perfect man, unto the measure of the age of the fulness of Christ"—the human race will have achieved its purpose as a race. All the men who are to be incorporated with Christ—built into his Body—will have been thus incorporated, and all will be completely one with him. Then will come the end of the world and the General Judgment. Christ will judge the whole world—all men will be in their place for all men to see—and the whole immense plan of God will be seen as a thing perfectly achieved. The bodies of men—glorified, as Christ's is—will be reunited with their souls; and every man—body and soul—will be forever established in joy or woe.

There roughly is the map. If it is a good map, a well-drawn map, then one should be able to find one's bearings by it—to find where one stands in relation to all other things, to find the end of the road and the way to it. So much a good map can do. The best map cannot do more. A map is concerned with the surface and cannot tell you in detail of the treasures that lie beneath. On the field here mapped, there is no point at which one may not dig with immeasurable profit; or to abandon the metaphor, every single truth mentioned is but a single name for a whole world of truth. The Blessed Trinity will yield truth for our meditation for all eternity, and even here below we shall not exhaust what here below may be known. Or if, leaving the intricacies of the map we concentrate on any one point of it—the excellence of our Lady, for instance, or the life of prayer—we shall come upon a mine of truth by comparison with which the bare outlines of a map may seem poor colourless things. But even for the appreciation of any one doctrine, the map is necessary. No truth is merely itself: something pours into it from all other truth; and for a study of any one point of revealed truth there is no better equipment than a general view of the whole.